Finding Your True North

ALSO BY BILL GEORGE

Authentic Leadership
True North

Warren Bennis

A WARREN BENNIS BOOK

This collection of books is devoted exclusively to new and exemplary contributions to management thought and practice. The books in this series are addressed to thoughtful leaders, executives, and managers of all organizations who are struggling with and committed to responsible change. My hope and goal is to spark new intellectual capital by sharing ideas positioned at an angle to conventional thought—in short, to publish books that disturb the present in the service of a better future.

Books in the Warren Bennis Signature Series

Finding Your True North

A Personal Guide

Bill George

Andrew N. McLean

Nick Craig

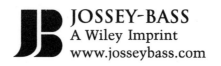

JOSSEY-BASS
A Wiley Imprint
www.josseybass.com

Published by Jossey-Bass
A Wiley Imprint
One Montgomery, Ste. 1200, San Francisco, CA 94104 —www.josseybass.com

Readers should be aware that Internet Web sites offered as citations and/or sources for further information may have changed or disappeared between the time this was written and when it is read.

Jossey-Bass books and products are available through most bookstores. To contact Jossey-Bass directly call our Customer Care Department within the U.S. at 800-956-7739, outside the U.S. at 317-572-3986, or fax 317-572-4002.

Jossey-Bass also publishes its books in a variety of electronic formats. Some content that appears in print may not be available in electronic books.

Library of Congress Cataloging-in-Publication Data

George, Bill (William W.)
    Finding your true north : a personal guide / Bill George, Andrew N. McLean, Nick Craig. — 1st ed.
        p. cm.
      ISBN 978-0-470-26136-1 (pbk.)
      1. Leadership. 2. Organizational effectiveness. I. McLean, Andrew N., 1966- II. Craig, Nick, 1960-
III. Title.
HD57.7.G45814 2008
658.4'092—dc22   2008009381

Printed in the United States of America
FIRST EDITION
PB Printing   10 9 8 7 6

Contents

Table of Exercises

Bill George dedicates this book to his wife, Penny, and his sons, Jeff and Jon,
and daughters-in-law, Renee and Jeannette,
all of whom are authentic leaders pursuing their own passions.

Andrew McLean dedicates this book to his wife, Kathleen, and his son Aidan,
in the hope that authentic leaders will make a difference in the world.

Nick Craig dedicates this book to the authentic leaders in his life,
who showed him the way by being just themselves.

Preface
Why a Personal Guide to *True North*?
by Bill George

Leadership matters. It matters a great deal—to our organizations and institutions, to the people who work in them, and to the people who are served by them. For our society to function effectively, we need authentic leaders who can encourage people to perform at their best and step up and lead themselves.

I wrote *True North* because I have a passion to see more people in all walks of life lead authentically and because I wanted to help people like you discover your authentic leadership.

Finding Your True North: A Personal Guide will enable you to take the ideas and lessons from the book *True North* and apply them to your personal leadership development. This will enable you to become a highly effective—and authentic—leader who knows your True North and stays on its course.

DISCOVERING YOUR AUTHENTIC LEADERSHIP

Becoming an authentic leader takes hard work. It is not much different from becoming a great musician or a great athlete. To become great in any endeavor—whether it is in your career, your family, or your community—you must use the unique strengths you were born with and develop them to the fullest, while acknowledging and learning from your shortcomings.

In my case, I had to work very hard to become a leader, enduring disappointing defeats and rejections in high school and early college years and searching for many years to find the right place to flourish as a leader. I had to make the "leadership journey into my own soul" that General Electric's Jeff Immelt describes in order to find out who I am, where my real passions lie, and how I could become more effective as a leader. I didn't have a personal guide like this one to help me, so I made up my development plan as I went along, with the help of my wife, close friends, and some important mentors along the way.

After searching for a role model for many years, I learned that I could never become a great leader by emulating someone else or by minimizing my shortcomings. As "Director of the Year" Reatha Clark King told me, "If you're aiming to be like somebody else, you're being a copycat because you think that's what people want you to do. You'll never be a star with that kind of thinking. But you might be a star—unreplicatable—by following your passion."

Many leadership books offer a quick fix to becoming a leader, or provide you with seven easy steps to leadership. Unfortunately, leadership development doesn't work that way, any more than you can become a great athlete by reading a book. To realize your potential as a leader, you need a detailed development program that will enable you to become an excellent leader. That's the purpose of *Finding Your True North:* to enable you to develop a clear and detailed program for your personal leadership development.

I encourage you to have as many leadership experiences early in life as you can. Don't sit back and wait for these experiences to come to you. Seek them out! After each experience, you should process them by going back to your development plan to see what changes you need to make or further experiences you should have.

Recall the fundamental messages from *True North:*

- *You can discover your authentic leadership right now.*
- *You do not have to be born with the characteristics or traits of a leader.*
- *You do not have to wait for a tap on your shoulder.*
- *You do not have to be at the top of your organization.*
- *You can step up to lead at any point in your life: you're never too young—or too old.*
- *Leadership is your choice, not your title.*

USING THIS PERSONAL GUIDE

Finding Your True North offers you a series of exercises that will enable you to go deeper into your life story, discover your passions, and develop into an authentic leader. It starts with an exploration of your life story and its relationship to your leadership. Then, you will examine the leadership experiences you have had thus far in your life, as well as your challenges and disappointments. You will have the opportunity to explore ways that you might get pulled off course from your True North.

After that, you will be ready to delve more deeply into the greatest crucible of your life and to understand and frame your experiences at a deeper level. This understanding can enable you to make the transformation from an "I" leader to a "We" leader.

Next you will go to work on the five key elements of your personal development as a leader: gaining self-awareness, clarifying your values and principles, understanding your motivations, building your support team, and leading an integrated life.

In the final section, you will author your leadership, exploring your leadership purpose, understanding how you can be an empowering leader, and examining ways to optimize your leadership effectiveness.

After completing this work, you are ready to create your Personal Leadership Development Plan (PLDP). This is a dynamic document that you can return to in future years to assess your progress, update your plan based on experiences since it was created, and prepare for the next phase of your leadership journey.

SHOULD I WORK WITH OTHERS WHILE USING THIS GUIDE?

Your responses to the exercises and your notes in this personal guide are your confidential work. However, we do encourage you to share them with others, including your trusted mentors, coaches, support team, and leadership discussion group. This feedback will be invaluable to you in developing your PLDP.

As you share yourself, your story, and your answers with others close to you, take the risk of revealing your vulnerabilities. You will find that sharing with others in this way is a very liberating experience. When you are open with others, they in turn will feel safe in being open with you, and you will form deeper bonds. There are several ways you can use this guide:

1. As an individual, you can do the exercises on your own and prepare your PLDP.

2. You can work through this personal guide as a group with friends or even new acquaintances, as each of you completes the exercises individually, discusses the results openly with the other members of the group, and solicits their feedback. Then it can be helpful to go back to the exercises and update them, based on the feedback.

   Your group can be led by a professional facilitator, who guides your discussion and keeps the group on track. Or you can create a peer-facilitated group, in which leadership of the group rotates to a different group member for each session. We have used this latter approach very successfully with six-person Leadership Discussion Groups (LDGs) in my Authentic Leadership Development classes at Harvard Business School. (See Appendix B for suggestions on forming such a group.)

3. To enhance your work on your leadership, you can use *Finding Your True North* under the guidance of a coach or mentor. Your coach or mentor can work with you on each of the exercises, give you valuable feedback, and encourage you to explore yourself and your story more deeply.

4. You can use this personal guide with your team at work. It will enable team members to discover their authentic leadership and help the team function more effectively because they understand each other better through sharing their stories. As team leader, you can guide your team through the process, or you can use a professional team-building consultant and facilitator.

5. You can use this guide along with *True North* as the basis for a course on leadership development, either in an academic setting or in an organization. It has the flexibility to be used with leaders at all stages in their careers: young leaders, including college and graduate students; midcareer leaders; leaders at the top of their organizations;

and leaders embarking on the third phase of their leadership journeys after they have completed their principle leadership roles.

In the case of a larger group, you will need a professor, teacher, or leadership development professional to structure the material and lead the group. Such a course should include the cases listed in Appendix C that were specifically developed for use in leadership development courses. In addition, it is highly recommended that your group be broken into smaller LDGs for discussion of more personal matters.

A FINAL WORD TO USERS OF THIS PERSONAL GUIDE

As you embark on discovering your authentic leadership by moving into the heart of this guide, let me offer my personal welcome to you in your desire to become an authentic leader and to follow your True North. I encourage you to be completely open and transparent as you look inside yourself and answer the very challenging and difficult questions posed in the exercises. Have the courage to explore your life story deeply to understand who you are as a human being, where you fit in this world, how you can use your leadership to impact the world in a positive way, and how you can leave a lasting legacy.

I am excited about the opportunity that you and thousands of leaders like you have to transform organizations and institutions in business, the nonprofit world, governments, education, and religion, as you bring authenticity to the workplace and encourage others to lead in the same way.

Your dedication to becoming an authentic leader will indeed make this world a better and richer place for all of us to live in.

February 2008

BILL GEORGE
MINNEAPOLIS

Introduction
Why Authentic Leadership Development?

> Something ignited in my soul. . . . And I went my
> own way, deciphering that burning fire.
> —*Pablo Neruda*

Why is it important for you to become an authentic leader?

There are many leaders who get ahead in organizations who are anything *but* authentic. You have certainly met them. They may be domineering people who use their power to rise up the ladder and are willing to take advantage of less powerful people to get ahead. They may be constantly directing, controlling, and dealing with others aggressively. Often they seem incapable of accepting honest feedback. Sometimes they willingly use other people to hit their numbers. They might stretch the truth or seize political advantage if it makes them look good. They are likely to make a lot of money on their way to fame and glory.

You could be this kind of leader.

"What's wrong with that?" you ask.

Plenty. Leaders like these cannot motivate people toward a common goal. They are incapable of building trust within organizations. In short, they are ineffective leaders.

Worse, leaders like this destroy good people. They destroy great organizations. Although they may be successful in the short term, over time their behavior catches up with them. Then they either move on or watch their organizations steadily decline.

Do you want to be an effective leader who can sustain success over an extended period of time? Then it is essential that you discover your authentic leadership. This personal guide will enable you to become an authentic—and effective—leader. It will help you understand your True North and develop a plan to stay on course, no matter how difficult the challenges you may face.

Before we dig into the details of *how* you can discover your authentic leadership, let's examine why being authentic is so essential to your effectiveness as a leader.

Leading in the twenty-first century is vastly different from leading in the twentieth century. People in organizations have changed dramatically—to the point where they will no longer tolerate or be motivated by the "command and control" leaders of the twentieth century. Nor will they be impressed by charismatic leaders who say one thing and do another.

Over the last fifty years, all of us followed powerful leaders who seemed to know where they were going, only to discover that often they were leading us down destructive paths. Or that these leaders were only out for themselves and were unconcerned with our well-being. Organizations expected us to be loyal to our leaders and wait in line for our turn to lead, if it ever came. And then we learned that our loyalty was not returned, as we witnessed many people lose their pensions and their health care. As a consequence, we lost trust in our leaders. In recent years, many of us were dazzled by charismatic leaders who impressed everyone with their charm, yet went off the deep end.

People in organizations today seek authentic leaders whom they can trust, but they are not so easily fooled or so quick to offer their loyalty. They are knowledge workers who often know more than their bosses. They want the opportunity to step up and lead now; they won't wait in line for ten to twenty years. If they can't find those opportunities, they are quite prepared to move on, as they have multiple options and refuse to get locked into negative situations. They are willing to work extremely hard, but will do so only for a cause they believe in, as they are seeking meaning and significance in their work. They are willing to trust their leaders only if these leaders prove themselves worthy of their trust.

If you want to be *effective* as a leader, then you must be an *authentic leader*. If you are not authentic, the best people won't want to work with you, and they won't give you their best work.

What does it take to be both authentic and effective as a leader?

- You must align people around a common purpose that inspires them to peak performance.

- You must unite them around a common set of values, so that people know precisely what is expected of them. You should serve as a role model for these values.

- You must empower people to step up and lead so that people throughout the organization are highly motivated and give their best to the organization.

- You must serve all your constituencies; as a leader, you bear the responsibility of serving your customers, employees, shareholders, and communities.

This is not easy. It is the hard side of leadership.

The easy side of leadership is getting the short-term numbers right. Lots of smart people can figure out how to do that. It is much more difficult to get people aligned, empowered, and committed to serve all their constituencies.

Being *authentic* as a leader creates a virtuous circle, as the best people will want to work with you. As a result, the performance of your teams will be superior, and you will be able to take on greater challenges.

The bottom line is this: in the twenty-first century, without authenticity in leadership, there will be no sustained effectiveness in organizations.

With authentic leadership, the potential for organizations to compete and to excel is unlimited.

WHAT IS AN AUTHENTIC LEADER?

Let's start by describing the authentic leader.

To be an authentic leader requires you to be genuine and to have a passion for your purpose; you must practice your values, lead with your heart, develop connected relationships, and have the self-discipline to get results. You must stay on course of your True North in the face of the most severe challenges, pressures, and seductions.

This means being true to yourself and to what you believe in, which will enable you to engender trust and develop genuine connections with others. Because people trust you, you will be able to motivate them to high levels of performance. Rather than letting the expectations of others guide you, you must be prepared to be your own person and go your own way. As you develop as an authentic leader, you will be more concerned about serving others than about your own success or recognition.

This does not mean you have to be perfect. Far from it. Like all of us, you can have your weaknesses and be subject to the full range of human frailties and mistakes, and still be an authentic leader. Yet by acknowledging your shortcomings and admitting your errors, you will connect with people and empower them.

Purpose

To find your purpose, you must first understand yourself and your passions. In turn, your passions show the way to the purpose of your leadership.

Values

As a leader, you are defined by your values, which are the deeply held beliefs that guide your actions. Your values are personal: they cannot be determined by anyone except you. To lead by your values is to give expression to your most deeply held beliefs through your leadership. The test of your values is not what you say, but how you behave under pressure. If you are not true to the values you profess, people will quickly lose confidence in your leadership.

Heart

As an authentic leader, you must lead with your heart as well as your head. This means having passion for your work, compassion for the people you serve, empathy for the people with whom you work, and the courage to make difficult decisions.

Connected Relationships

To lead with connected relationships is to develop long-lasting and enduring connections with other people in all types of relationships. Connected relationships enable you to build trust and commitment through the openness and depth of your relationships, and to engender commitment from people.

Self-Discipline

Competing successfully takes a consistently high level of self-discipline on your part in order to produce results. Such discipline enables you to set high standards for yourself and to hold others accountable for their performance. When you fall short—and you will—it is equally important to admit your mistakes and initiate immediate corrective action.

HOW WILL THIS BOOK HELP YOU BECOME AN AUTHENTIC LEADER?

To develop as an authentic leader, you start with your own experiences and your life story as grounding and inspiration for your leadership. You identify your present leadership development profile by reviewing your experiences in order to learn from them. You examine the reasons why leaders lose their way by being an imposter, rationalizer, glory seeker, loner, or shooting star, and how this might happen to you as well. You explore the greatest crucible of your life and discover how it impacts your leadership. These elements are covered in Part One of this personal guide.

Part Two turns to leadership development by focusing on the elements of the True North compass:

- *Leading with purpose* requires self-awareness—the cornerstone of authentic leadership development.
- *Leading through values* comes through developing clarity about your values, leadership principles, and ethical boundaries.

- *Leading with heart* comes through understanding your motivations and finding the sweet spot where your motivations mesh with your greatest capabilities.

- *Leading through connected relationships* comes through the development of a personal support team.

- *Leading with self-discipline* comes through the integration of one's life.

Part Three focuses on authentic leadership in action. It moves from leading with purpose to empowering others in your organization, and finally to optimiz-

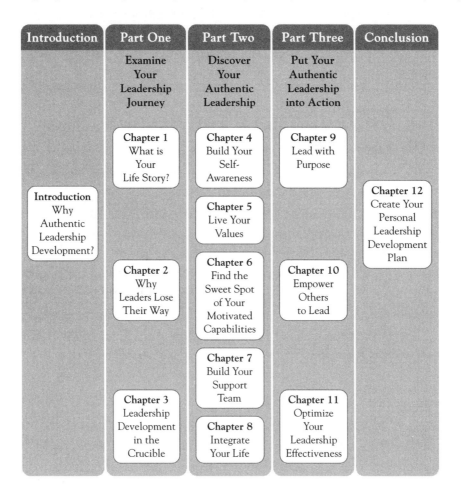

Introduction	Part One	Part Two	Part Three	Conclusion
	Examine Your Leadership Journey	Discover Your Authentic Leadership	Put Your Authentic Leadership into Action	
	Chapter 1 What is Your Life Story?	**Chapter 4** Build Your Self-Awareness	**Chapter 9** Lead with Purpose	
Introduction Why Authentic Leadership Development?		**Chapter 5** Live Your Values		**Chapter 12** Create Your Personal Leadership Development Plan
	Chapter 2 Why Leaders Lose Their Way	**Chapter 6** Find the Sweet Spot of Your Motivated Capabilities	**Chapter 10** Empower Others to Lead	
		Chapter 7 Build Your Support Team		
	Chapter 3 Leadership Development in the Crucible	**Chapter 8** Integrate Your Life	**Chapter 11** Optimize Your Leadership Effectiveness	

ing the effectiveness of your leadership through appropriate use of style and power. In conclusion, you will bring together all you have learned from the exercises that you worked on in this guide to prepare your Personal Leadership Development Plan.

Authentic leaders can take their leadership to a higher level of performance because they inspire confidence, trust, and loyalty in their organization and in their work. They have an advantage in aligning others around a common purpose, empowering other leaders, and using the full range of their leadership capabilities.

YOUR IDEA OF LEADERSHIP

Finding Your True North is for all leaders, regardless of what group or organization you lead, whether you have already established your leadership and are trying to develop yourself further, if you plan to be a leader in the future, or even if you don't usually think of yourself as a leader.

Consider these contrasting examples:

"From my earliest days I have been fascinated with leadership," said Kevin Sharer, CEO of Amgen. "When somebody asked me at ten years old, 'What do you want to do when you grow up?' I said, 'I just want to be in charge.'"

"I don't think other people think of me as a leader," said David Kelley, founder of IDEO. "'Leader' is a funny word for me. You see, I'm a collaborator. If there is a problem, I call all the smart people I know and get them in a room and have them figure it out."

How about you? How do you think of yourself as a leader?

The truth is, these leaders are constantly leading and working on developing themselves as leaders, regardless of what they label themselves. We have learned from many leaders like them that the process of developing their authentic leadership is quite similar, although the expression of each person's leadership is unique.

INTRODUCTORY EXERCISE 1:
LEADERSHIP IMAGES IN MY LIFE

You first encounter leadership and leaders through the examples of others. These examples give you patterns from which to learn. They are the raw material from which you build the conceptions of leadership you carry into your work and your life.

The purpose of this exercise is to draw on the thinking that you have already done on the topic of leadership. The exercise starts with your existing models of leadership.

Think of five leaders, past or present, whom you have admired. Write their names below, and then answer for yourself the questions that follow.

1. Dick Blake
2. Andrea Salazar
3. Ghandi
4. Alberto Cuitiño
5. Ed McNeil

Which of these leaders have had the greatest impact on my idea of leadership?

1. Andrea Salazar
2. Alberto Cuitiño
3. Ed McNeil

What specific examples of leadership stand out in my mind for each of these leaders?

1.
2.
3.
4.
5.

Which three of these leaders do I consider to be authentic leaders?

1. _Ghandi_
2. _Martin Luther King_
3. _____

What reservations or concerns might I have about following each one?

1. _Ghandi → The courage to follow_
2. _MLK → non-violence_
3. _____

How did the context of the leaders I identified differ from what I face in my life today?

1. _I do not fear my well being as they did_
2. _The change they sought was far greater + important_
3. _____

What qualities, if any, of these three leaders would I like to emulate?

1. _Their ability to communicate well to the masses_
2. _They make their purpose easy to understand_
3. _They had clear instructions_

What qualities, if any, would I like to avoid?

1. _____
2. _____
3. _____

NO LEADER IS PERFECT

The biographies of those most often placed on the "best leaders" lists can be surprising at times. Even the most widely admired leaders have very human weaknesses: notable failures as well as successes, startling inconsistencies in relationships or behaviors, times of intense struggle with their values and principles. These shortcomings do not disqualify any leader from being a source of inspiration, a role model for others, or a teacher. Indeed, effective leadership teachers and mentors must know and understand their own developmental needs in order to help you work on yours.

INTRODUCTORY EXERCISE 2: MY PREPARATION FOR LEADERSHIP

The purpose of this exercise is to establish your starting point for your work with this personal guide.

What are the most important qualities I bring to leadership?

1. Listening Skills
2. Intelligence
3. Work Ethic
4.
5.

All good leaders are continuously developing. Which of my leadership qualities would I like to develop further?

1. Inexperience
2. Prioritizing what is important.
3. Public Speaking.
4.
5.

It is important to keep in mind the leadership qualities that you would like to develop. This book is intended to help you fulfill your aspirations to become an authentic and effective leader as you stay on the course of your True North. No one can give you the leadership qualities you seek. You already have those leadership qualities within you. This guide is designed to help you bring out those qualities and put them into your everyday practice of leadership.

LEARNING FROM YOUR LEADERSHIP JOURNEY

In Part One, you will begin working with the story of your leadership journey. You will go beyond the standard signposts of leadership by looking through the lens of your life story, learning from times when you lost your way, and examining the greatest crucible of your life.

KEY TAKE-AWAYS

- Being authentic is essential to your effectiveness as a leader.
- To be an effective leader, you need to develop the five dimensions of the authentic leader.
- Your leadership is unique because it is grounded in your life story and your experiences in leading.
- Becoming an authentic leader requires that you undertake a disciplined process of personal development.

SUGGESTED READING

Bennis, W. *On Becoming a Leader.* Reading, Mass.: Addison-Wesley, 1989.

Boyatzis, R., and McKee, A. *Resonant Leadership.* Boston: Harvard Business School Press, 2005.

Collins, J. *Good to Great.* New York: HarperCollins, 2002.

Gardner, J. *On Leadership.* New York: Free Press, 1990.

Kanter, R. *America the Principled.* New York: Crown Books, 2007.

Kopp, W. *One Day, All Children . . .* Cambridge, Mass.: Perseus Press, 2003.

Finding Your True North

Part One

Examine Your Leadership Journey

When you're in trouble and all your defenses get stripped away,
you realize what matters and who matters. That's when you
need to get back to your roots and to your values.
—*David Gergen, counselor to four U.S. presidents*

Your life story is the foundation for your leadership. Your development as an authentic leader begins by analyzing your life story and your formative experiences. As you learn from your past experiences, you will be able to develop tools to see yourself clearly, understand your leadership achievements, and embrace your goals for future leadership development.

In Part One of this guide, we will begin with your life story.

1

What Is Your Life Story?

We are the mosaic of all our experiences.
—*Kevin Sharer, chairman and CEO, Amgen*

The process of becoming a True North leader starts with discovering your leadership gifts by understanding your unique life story.

In this chapter you have the opportunity to look back at your life story and understand the important elements in your experience. You will be exploring how they fit together to define you as a unique individual and provide your capacity to lead. This is the starting point for gaining greater self-awareness and for understanding what your life and your leadership are all about.

During the 125 interviews we conducted with authentic leaders for *True North*, these leaders consistently told us that they found their purpose for leadership through understanding their life stories. Their stories enabled them to remain grounded in who they are and stay focused on their True North.

These leaders did not define themselves by their characteristics, traits, or styles. Although some tried to emulate great leaders early in their lives, they soon learned that emulating someone else's leadership did not result in their becoming effective leaders.

Some interviewees did not see themselves as leaders at all, even though they had been identified by others as exemplary leaders. Instead, they viewed themselves as people who wanted to make a difference and who inspired others to join with them in pursuing common goals. By understanding and framing their life stories, they found their passion to lead and were able to discover their True North. As a result, they were able to sustain their leadership purpose, achieve lasting success, and realize the fulfillment of leadership.

EXERCISE 1.1: MY PATH OF LIFE

In this first exercise, you are going to draw the path of your life to date, like the example you see in Figure 1.1. On the facing page is a workspace for drawing your own path of life. Label the lower left corner of the page "Birth" and the upper right "Present Day." Begin to draw the path of your life from one corner to the other.

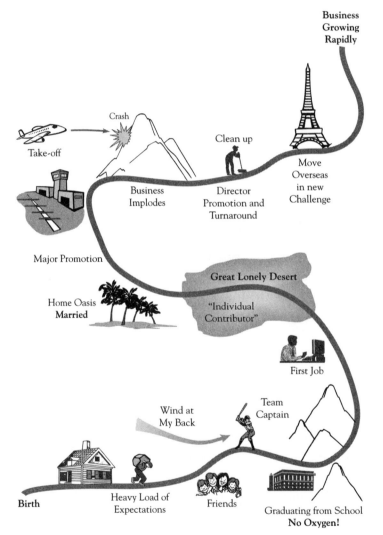

Figure 1.1 Path of Life Example

Your Path of Life

Let the terrain of your path be unique to who you are. Include mountains and valleys, cities and wilderness, forks, bridges, cliffs.

Add in houses, buildings, and so on along the path, representing places you have lived. Likewise, indicate key people and key events with pictures or a diagram along or across the path.

Add representations of your family, your work, your spiritual life, other life pursuits you have had . . . anything that is meaningful to you.

Be creative and allow your story to unfold in front of you.

Looking at the path, divide your life story into four or five chapters marked by major changes or transitions in your life. Give each chapter a descriptive title and add it to your path.

LEARNING FROM YOUR LIFE STORY

Stories are the way you capture your experiences in a form that you can understand and that you can communicate to others. There are three elements to bear in mind about the life story work in this personal guide.

First, the story you have to tell depends on the point of view you take in regard to it. For our purposes, it is sufficient to draw the distinctions between telling your story as a hero, a victim, or a knowledgeable bystander. Your story work will be most helpful if you cultivate the perspective of a knowledgeable bystander rather than that of a hero or a victim. If you are a hero, you will miss out on what you need to work on. As a victim, you will miss out on your strengths. As a knowledgeable bystander, you can be your own friend or mentor who won't pull any punches, but who is definitely on your side.

Second, your story may change dramatically depending on the time that has passed since it happened and the situation you are in when you tell it. When telling the story of your leadership, try to relate both the long sequence of events and all the smaller details you remember. Do your best to tell the story from start to finish so that you can capture the heart of each episode.

Third, a story differs depending on whether you are seeking balance and resolution in telling the story or are cultivating a dialogue and opening up points of tension. Telling the story of your struggle to make a leadership decision can capture the uncertainties and possibilities in your leadership that remain to be resolved. We are all trained to tell stories that give closure and resolution. When it comes to the story of your leadership development, it is unlikely that there will be a clear resolution. But the messy, problematic aspects of your story may be the most interesting and useful in thinking about where your life experiences are leading you.

Now let's shift our focus to the life story of the most important leader in your life: **you.**

EXERCISE 1.2: LEARNING ABOUT MY LEADERSHIP

Reviewing your Path of Life, think back over all your leadership experiences in your lifetime. Choose the leadership experience of which you are proudest. In this exercise, put yourself back in that time and describe it as if it were happening to you right now.

Describe your proudest leadership experience, starting with the specific events.

What happened?

_____

_____

_____

_____

_____

What was the history or climate of the organization I was in?

_____

_____

_____

What triggered the experience? What caused me to step up and lead?

_____

_____

_____

What was the outcome? What changed in the people in the organization as a result?

_____

_____

_____

How did I feel . . .

Before stepping up to lead?

_____

When I first stepped up to lead?

_____

When facing the challenges of the situation?

_____

After the results were in?

_____

What things did I just learn about my leadership as I told this story?

1. _____

2. _____

3. _____

Telling your story is an important part of authentic leadership development. Writing your story down gives you a point of reference and helps you gain perspective on yourself.

Now let's probe more deeply into your experience so that you can gain even greater insight into your own story.

What leadership qualities did I bring to that leadership experience?

1. _____
2. _____
3. _____
4. _____
5. _____

How did those qualities contribute to the outcome? Link an outcome to each of the qualities you listed above.

My Leadership Quality	Its Effect on the Outcome
1.	
2.	
3.	
4.	
5.	

Draw on what you have read in *True North* about the dimensions of authentic leadership. Referring to the experience you just related, rate yourself on the following statements using a 1–5 scale (1 = Not at all and 5 = Very strongly):

Dimension	Rating
I understood my purpose.	
I practiced my values.	
I understood my motivations.	
I used my support team.	
I was an integrated leader.	

Now, be your own mentor.

Turn back to this story again and look at it from the perspective of the leader you have become since that time.

If I were mentoring myself at that time, what advice would I give?

_____

_____

_____

In the same spirit, make a list for yourself.

One thing I did really well:

_____

One thing I could have done better:

_____

One thing I could try next time:

_____

In this exercise, you've taken an important step in understanding who you are as a leader and what is important and effective in your leadership. You have thought about what happened, who you were then, and how you can learn from that peak leadership experience.

AUTHENTICITY AND EFFECTIVENESS

How are authenticity and effectiveness related? You may worry that by being truly authentic in the workplace you will sacrifice the performance edge that has gotten you this far. You may be concerned about deviating from expected norms, or not being recognized as a leader. You may worry that you will be exposed to disappointment when you put yourself on the line and things do not work out. These are understandable concerns. There are many constraining models of leadership that discourage us from exploring our authentic leadership.

We have found that authentic leaders inspire trust and loyalty. They perform at superior levels because they are intensely focused on a powerful purpose for their leadership. They are also able to remain grounded through success or failure. By being committed, they are able to pick themselves up and keep moving even after the most devastating setbacks. Next we will explore the relationship between your authenticity and your effectiveness.

EXERCISE 1.3: AUTHENTICITY AND LEADERSHIP EFFECTIVENESS

The purpose of this exercise is to take stock of how you think authenticity affects your leadership.

I have the following thoughts about being both authentic and effective as a leader:

1. _____

2. _____

3. _____

How does being authentic make me more effective right now?

1. _____

2. _____

3. _____

YOUR JOURNEY TO AUTHENTIC LEADERSHIP

Experience is often said to be the best teacher. Experience is, however, not necessarily a kind or clear teacher. Your life story is in part a chronicle of your experiences in the world. Looking at earlier and later chapters, you will notice contrasts. In one chapter, you may have been preparing to lead. In another, you may have focused on leading or simply trying to make your way in the world. Some passages may be marked by education or apprenticeship—times when you were operating in the context of rules that structured and measured your activities. Later chapters may come in a different context, perhaps marked by increased responsibilities and fewer rules and structures.

The interesting thing is that most post-education experiences are perceived as learning experiences only in retrospect. At any given moment, you will probably not have the feeling that you are preparing or training. You will be in the thick of your life. If you pay attention to the possibilities in each situation or crisis, however, every day can be a lesson on your journey to True North.

Now let's look at your leadership story from another perspective. Whereas you told the previous story as if you were experiencing it in real time, now you are going to tell this story from satellite height, surveying the whole story of your life and leadership. This story does not need to be bounded by what many leaders conventionally think of as their career or work-related life. Through our interviews we learned that the pre-career years of a leader's life were frequently the most formative and were often the most significant contributors to both the type of leaders they became and the formation of their True North.

EXERCISE 1.4: MY LIFE STORY

In this exercise, you will be looking at each of the chapters in your life story to identify the people, events, and experiences that have had the greatest impact on your life.

Start by looking back at the chapters you identified in your path of life (Exercise 1.1).

What people, events, and experiences have had the greatest impact on my life?

_____

_____

_____

_____

_____

Consider each chapter in turn, and use the following questions to guide yourself through a process of identifying key trends in your leadership story. Use the list generated above in this exercise and the path of life you drew previously, and also include anything else that occurs to you now.

Begin with your Chapter 1 and use the prompts in Table 1.1 as a guide.

Table 1.1: The Impact of My Life Story

	Chapter 1	Chapter 2	Chapter 3	Chapter 4	Chapter 5
Chapter title					
The experiences in this chapter made me believe . . .					
The experiences in this chapter made me more or less . . .					
If I could go back, these are the things I would have more or less of in this chapter:					
I am affected by what happened in this chapter on a daily basis in these ways:					

Now you are going to look at your story as a whole.

Where do my inspiration and passion for leadership appear first in my story?

_____

_____

_____

How have they developed over time?

_____

_____

_____

Look in particular at the people in your life story. Consider the impact parents, siblings and family members, mentors, and friends had on your inspiration and passion for leadership.

Who had the greatest influences on my leadership?

_____

_____

_____

Look at major experiences in your life story. Consider the influence of early leadership experiences in school, in sports, in your community, or at work.

How have my major leadership experiences influenced my leadership?

_____

_____

_____

How did the events, experiences, transitions, crises, and success within each chapter affect me as a person?

_____

_____

_____

When was I dissatisfied with my leadership, or when did I receive constructive feedback from others about it?

In what situations did I find the greatest fulfillment in leading?

BUILDING ON YOUR STORY

In this chapter, you have started to discover your gifts for leadership by understanding your life story. Laying your whole life out in front of you can be a powerful experience. Rarely do we step back and see the journey we are on. Through the lens of your life story, you can begin to see the wellsprings of your purpose, values, and motivations as a leader. Some of these have come from your proudest leadership experience; others may be speaking to you from major events in your life that defined who you are but seem to have no direct bearing on leadership. Thus you are probably starting to see how your leadership relates to both your work life and your nonwork life.

In the next chapter, you will look deeper into your story. You will begin working on what may initially be uncomfortable subjects: the hazards of leadership and the lessons of adversity. You will find that revisiting difficult experiences and exploring leadership hazards can bring both insight and clarity to your True North.

KEY TAKE-AWAYS

- Learning from the experiences in your life story holds the key to your development as a leader.

- To learn best from your story, it is important to step away both from the hero's and from the victim's view of your story, and to be an objective observer of yourself.

- Your past leadership experiences point the way to discovering your potential as an authentic leader.

- Each chapter of your life story carries critical lessons that will help you find *your* True North.

SUGGESTED READING

Baldwin, C. *Storycatcher: How the Power of Story Can Change Our Lives*. Novato, Calif.: New World Library, 2005.

Bstan-dzin-rgya-mtsho, Dalai Lama XIV. *A Simple Path*. (G. T. Jinpa, trans.). London: Thorsons, 2000.

Damasio, A. *Descartes' Error*. New York: Vintage, 2006.

Franco, C., and Lineback, K. *The Legacy Guide: Capturing the Facts, Memories, and Meaning of Your Life*. New York: Penguin, 2006.

Gibran, K. *The Prophet*. New York: Knopf, 1951. (Originally published 1923.)

Komisar, R. *The Monk and the Riddle: The Education of a Silicon Valley Entrepreneur*. Boston: Harvard Business School Press, 2000.

Michelli, J. *The Starbucks Experience*. New York: McGraw-Hill, 2006.

Sonnenfeld, J. *The Hero's Farewell*. New York: Oxford University Press, 1988.

2

Why Leaders Lose Their Way

In the middle of the road of my life, I awoke in a dark wood,
Where the true way was wholly lost.
—*Dante*, The Divine Comedy

Leadership development is a journey through challenging terrain. All leaders, including the most authentic ones, face significant hazards on their journeys. Being human, leaders seek rewards for themselves, avoid negative consequences, and seek social acceptance and approbation. These are normal human tendencies, but they can sabotage a leader's personal and professional achievements.

Authentic leaders must learn to be aware of and overcome the personal impulses that lead to problematic behaviors. Leaders who lose their way succumb to the negative temptations of leadership and may even celebrate these destructive tendencies.

The good news is that developing leaders can make mistakes and fall prey to these hazards, but still regain their footing and continue on their leadership journeys. In fact, their mistakes, especially those that come early in their careers, can be important drivers of their developmental process and reduce the likelihood of making major mistakes when they reach positions of authority. If emerging leaders are aware of the hazards and willing to devote sufficient time to their personal development, they will be less likely to become enmeshed in destructive patterns and more likely to persevere and emerge as authentic leaders.

ON THE HERO'S JOURNEY

Through our research on authentic leaders, we saw a striking feature of their stories. The early chapters of leaders' stories fit the pattern of what mythologist

Joseph Campbell has called "the Hero's Journey." Many leaders approach their early career as if they were on the quest of an all-conquering hero, with a primary focus on themselves—their skills, performance, achievements, and rewards.

The hero's job—doing impressive deeds, facing challenges alone, and gaining notice—may initially seem the best route to success. But acting as a hero is only a stage that authentic leaders move through on their journey to authentic leadership. It is a necessary but temporary stage—one with its own risks, temptations, and misbehaviors—and one that needs to be outgrown.

Falling into the Trap of Becoming a Hero

Many of the perils of the hero stage are well described by Daniel Vasella, CEO of Novartis, in a *Fortune* magazine interview:

> Once you get under the domination of making the quarter—even unwittingly . . . you'll begin to sacrifice things that are important and may be vital for your company over the long term. The culprit that drives this cycle isn't the fear of failure so much as it is the craving for success. . . . For many of us the idea of being a successful manager is an intoxicating one. It is a pattern of celebration leading to belief, leading to distortion. When you achieve good results, you are typically celebrated, and you begin to believe that the figure at the center of all that champagne toasting is yourself. You are idealized by the outside world, and there is a natural tendency to believe that what is written is true.

Leaf, C. "Temptation Is All Around Us." *Fortune*, Nov. 18, 2002

After moving through the hero stage, you can enter into the first stage of true leadership. Leaders who move beyond the hero stage learn to focus on others, gain a sense of a larger purpose, foster multiple support networks, and develop mechanisms to keep perspective and stay grounded. They become the kind of people employees and peers trust and want to work with.

During the hero stage of leadership development, you are particularly vulnerable to the five hazards discussed in this chapter. Yet whether you are in the hero stage or are already in later stages, the hazards persist.

THE HAZARDS OF LEADERSHIP DEVELOPMENT

The five perils of the leadership journey—distinctive destructive behaviors that tend to take root in the hero stage of managers' early career—include being an imposter; rationalizing; glory seeking; playing the loner; and being a shooting star. We all see these archetypes in others. The key is recognizing them in ourselves and through our stories.

To some extent, these hazards result from natural fears that developing leaders face as they pursue their leadership development. Table 2.1 illustrates some of these goals and the natural fears that come with them. For each fear, we have outlined both a destructive response and a healthy response.

In the sections that follow, we look at each of the hazards in turn.

Being an Imposter

When you feel like an imposter, it is difficult to act decisively, and you may experience paralyzing doubt. Your subsequent inaction may lead to poor results and external challenges. If you do not face and overcome this hazard, you will likely be tempted to attack your critics and cut yourself off from internal feedback. Because they are frustrated by their inability to influence you, your most competent subordinates may move on to greener pastures. Meanwhile, people remaining in the organization may be those who tend to keep their heads down and wait for you to make decisions.

Leaders are vulnerable to becoming imposters if they lack self-awareness. Having acquired power, imposters are not confident about how to use it. They are beset with doubts about handling the responsibilities of leadership. Because one of the strengths of their leadership is besting internal opponents, imposters may become paranoid that underlings are out to get them.

Table 2.1: Healthy Versus Destructive Responses to Normal Goals and Fears

Normal Goal	Natural Fear	Destructive Response	Healthy Response
Wanting respect and rewards from authority figures	Making mistakes and having one's lack of skill or knowledge exposed	Imposter (work with "Build Your Self-Awareness")	Self-led leader
Wanting things to go well	Getting blamed and suffering consequences	Rationalizer (work with "Live Your Values")	Straight shooter
Enjoying shared successes	Not being rewarded enough	Glory seeker (work with "Find the Sweet Spot of Your Motivated Capabilities")	"We"-focused leader
Thriving in interdependent relationships	Becoming too dependent on others	Loner (work with "Build Your Support Team")	Team-leader
Wanting to capitalize on successes for advancement	Falling behind others	Shooting star (work with "Integrate Your Life")	Rising star

Almost everyone experiences doubt about how to handle situations and feels the need to outshine others in order to rise in an organization. Worrying about your abilities, questioning whether you can handle a new challenge by yourself, sometimes having to display public confidence when you have private doubts, or recognizing your need to develop additional areas of knowledge and skill can all be characteristics of healthy, authentic leadership. It is when this doubt becomes your driving force that the problems begin.

The Imposter

Imposters frequently lack self-awareness and self-esteem. They may have little appetite for self-reflection and consequently defer personal development. They rise through the organizational ranks with a combination of cunning and aggression. Imposters use these strategies to achieve positions of power, but then have little sense of how to use that power for the good of the organization. In effect, they have been too busy besting competitors to learn how to lead. Leaders who succumb to this hazard embrace the politics of getting ahead and letting no one stand in their way. They are the ultimate political animals, adept at figuring out who their competitors are and then eliminating them one by one.

EXERCISE 2.1: IDENTIFYING THE IMPOSTER IN ME

This exercise focuses on recognizing aspects of the imposter in your life story.

Describe a situation where you found it difficult to make leadership decisions because of self-doubt.

_____

_____

_____

What did I think I was not able to do?

_____

_____

_____

What did I feel like? What did I feel my colleagues' response would be if I failed?

_____

_____

_____

How did I deal with the situation?

_____

_____

_____

What would I do differently today if I found myself in a similar position?

_____

_____

_____

In this exercise, you have identified an episode in your leadership journey when you faced a major challenge to your self-awareness. We have never met leaders who were not well acquainted with self-doubt and tempted at times to represent themselves as different from who they really were.

In Table 2.2, circle any of the characterizations that you identify with your present leadership.

Table 2.2: Indicators of the Imposter in Me

Healthy Approaches to Dealing with Doubt	*Early Warning Signs*	*Red Alerts*
I make the best decisions possible in a timely fashion.	My decision making becomes protracted as I seek perfect solutions.	I experience paralyzing doubt in business decisions.
I measure my capabilities against those needed to achieve my goals.	I measure competitors' capabilities rather than my own.	Political infighting takes priority over developing myself.
I seek actionable and appropriate developmental feedback.	I put off seeking feedback.	I am hostile to developmental feedback.
I take input from subordinates, peers, and superiors and then make my own best decision.	I seek input only when I know what I'm going to hear.	I am cut off from input from others.

If you circled examples in the Early Warning and Red Alert columns, you will want to pay particular attention to Chapter Four, "Build Your Self-Awareness," in Part Two.

Rationalizing

When you are being drawn off course by rationalizing, you tend to blame external forces or subordinates when things do not go your way. At first, you may deny that the problems actually exist. When you do acknowledge their existence and your responsibility for them, your instinct may be cover up the problems or seek to diminish their seriousness. You may not be willing to acknowledge even to yourself that things could get worse. If rationalizing becomes a habit, it is progressively more difficult to step up and take responsibility for the problems. In times like these, subordinates judge the values of their leaders and determine whether they are true to what they say they believe.

If you continue to rationalize outcomes, others in your organization may begin to rationalize their problems rather than facing up to them. The impact may spread throughout your group or organization. If it does, holding anyone accountable will become difficult. At that point, you may start to transmit greater pressure to subordinates instead of modulating it appropriately. When increased pressure fails to produce the desired results, you may resort to short-term strategies, such as cutting funding for research, growth initiatives, or organization building in order to hit immediate goals. You may be tempted to borrow from the future to make today's numbers look good, or to stretch accounting rules. You might justify these moves by believing you can make it up in the future. Ultimately, leaders who do not overcome the hazard of rationalizing become victims of their own rationalizations.

Leaders who are not clear about their values, leadership principles, and ethical boundaries are vulnerable to the hazards of rationalization. Lacking that clarity, they do not have sound boundaries around their behaviors, and may convince themselves that the ends justify the means. But, ultimately, the ends are not achieved, and the means do not constitute authentic leadership.

It is very difficult to consistently live up to your values and aspirations as a leader. All leaders have to make tough choices between competing values, and no one gets it right all the time. Weighing competing values or principles, taking the time to clarify a situation, and understanding that you and your colleagues struggle to make the best choices are characteristics of authentic leaders. But if this process turns into rationalizing, you may lose your way.

The Rationalizer

Rationalizers are unable to admit their mistakes for fear of being considered a failure or of losing their job. As a result of their inability to take responsibility for setbacks and failures, they rationalize their problems away, instead of facing reality. Their rationalizations lead to distortions and permit others to rationalize as well.

EXERCISE 2.2: IDENTIFYING THE RATIONALIZER IN ME

This exercise focuses on identifying times in your experiences when you rationalized your behavior.

Describe a situation where you rationalized failing to live up to your values.

_____

_____

_____

_____

_____

What were the values I was working around?

_____

_____

_____

How did I feel at the time?

_____

_____

_____

What happened as a result?

_____

_____

_____

If I found myself in a similar position today, what would I do in order to act differently?

_____

_____

_____

In Table 2.3, circle any of the characterizations that you identify with your present leadership.

If you circled examples in the Early Warning and Red Alert columns, you will want to pay particular attention to Chapter Five, "Live Your Values," in Part Two.

Glory Seeking

Glory seekers are leaders who are more concerned with their status and reputation than they are with building teams or organizations that create sustainable value.

You are at risk of becoming a glory seeker when you are motivated primarily by money, fame, power, and glory. If you let the external world define your success, and have a hunger for such recognition, you may find that your inner drive is constantly focused on obtaining more—more money, more adulation, more recognition, more prestige, or more power over others.

Table 2.3: Indicators of the Rationalizer in Me

Healthy Approaches to Making Difficult Decisions	Early Warning Signs	Red Alerts
I accept mixed outcomes from my decisions.	I often find it difficult to learn from mistakes and move on.	I am unable to acknowledge mistakes.
I weigh means and ends when making decisions.	I push the envelope of acceptable ways to achieve a goal.	I will do anything to achieve my goals; the ends justify the means.
I take appropriate risks, and find that some opportunities pass me by.	I borrow from the future to make ends meet because I take inappropriate risks	I have put others at risk in order to achieve a personal goal.
I occasionally operate in crisis mode.	I operate best in crisis mode.	I operate in continual states of crisis requiring short-term strategies.
I take responsibility for mistakes and fix them, encouraging others to do the same.	I find that problems and mistakes are orphans, without clear responsibility.	I operate in an accountability vacuum.
I communicate about both my challenges and my achievements.	I polish the upside to distract from problems.	I hide problems and bury bodies.

Glory seeking is the shadow expression of leaders who do not balance their intrinsic and extrinsic motivations and fail to link their motivations with their capabilities. It often results from a lack of self-love and a need to use external recognition to fill the void within.

The Glory Seeker

Leaders who seek glory are motivated by extrinsic motivations, such as a need for acclaim. The hazard of being derailed by glory seeking stems from these leaders' need for external reinforcement of their self-worth. Money, fame, glory, and power are their goals, as they pursue visible signs of success.

EXERCISE 2.3: IDENTIFYING THE GLORY SEEKER IN ME

This exercise focuses on identifying times in your life story when you behaved like a glory seeker.

Describe a situation when you felt an overwhelming need for external recognition or financial rewards to enhance your self-worth.

_____

_____

_____

What did it feel like at the time?

_____

_____

_____

How did I deal with my desires for glory?

_____

_____

_____

What would I do today if I found myself in a similar position?

_____

_____

_____

In Table 2.4, circle any of the characterizations that you identify with your present leadership.

If you circled examples in the Early Warning and Red Alert columns, you will want to pay particular attention to Chapter Six, "Find the Sweet Spot of Your Motivated Capabilities," in Part Two.

Table 2.4: Indicators of the Glory Seeker in Me

Healthy Approaches to Seeking Rewards from Your Work	Early Warning Signs	Red Alerts
I maintain a balanced portfolio of desires and motivations.	I have difficulty weighing tangible against intangible desires and motivations.	I choose fame, power, or glory over any other motivation.
I take on even drudge work in order to achieve my goals.	I defer meaningful or satisfying motivations out of necessity.	I find myself burned out and lacking in motivation to work.
I work toward shared goals with others, even when those goals are not all my own.	I work with others toward goals so long as those goals match my own.	I do not work with others because they do not have my interests at heart.
I ensure that others get appropriate credit for their contributions to my success.	I let others look out for their own credit for their contributions to my success.	I overstate my contributions to my success.

Being a Loner

You know you are falling into the trap of being a loner when you tend to avoid forming close relationships, do not seek out mentors, and do not have a support network of friends, colleagues, or peers. Being a loner is endemic among many leaders we have encountered. Many leaders are promoted to positions of increased power by relying on their individual capabilities, ambition, and a drive that may be born out of insecurity.

It is natural in the heroic stage of the leadership journey to think of leadership as a solitary pursuit, but it is also perilous. In a competitive world where leaders are evaluated on their individual merits, it stands to reason that aspiring leaders would take care to develop their own resources, husband their own ideas, and trust only their own judgment.

But therein lies the danger, as loners can easily fall into a self-reinforcing trap. Under pressure, they may retreat to the bunker when results are elusive and criticism of their leadership surfaces. As loners, they have few personal support structures in place to enable them to get through challenging times. As a result, they can become rigid in pursuing objectives, not recognizing that being a loner is making it impossible for them to reach their goals. Meanwhile, their teams and organizations can unravel, and their personal lives are at risk of crumbling, just when these leaders most need the support of family members.

The Loner

When leaders become loners, they cut themselves off from much-needed feedback. Yet without wise counsel, loners are prone to losing perspective and becoming rigid, which will lead to major mistakes.

EXERCISE 2.4: IDENTIFYING THE LONER IN ME

This exercise focuses on identifying times in your life when you acted like a loner in your leadership.

Describe a situation when you retreated into yourself rather than accessing the resources around you for counsel and advice.

_____

_____

_____

What did I feel at the time?

_____

_____

_____

How did I deal with the feelings of isolation and stress?

_____

_____

_____

What would I do differently now in order not to be so isolated if I found myself confronted by a similar situation?

_____

_____

_____

In Table 2.5, circle any of the characterizations that you identify with your present leadership.

If you circled examples in the Early Warning and Red Alert columns, you will want to pay particular attention to Chapter Seven, "Build Your Support Team," in Part Two.

Table 2.5: Indicators of the Loner in Me

Healthy Approaches to Interdependency	*Early Warning Signs*	*Red Alerts*
I seek input from others and then make up my own mind.	I avoid input from others and avoid working with groups or sharing responsibilities.	I do not accept input from others.
I take input and gauge the wind, but then look only forward after I make decisions.	I make impulsive decisions that seem to come out of the blue.	I make impulsive decisions that are out of touch with others in my organization.
I have a mix of long-term and short-term work relationships.	I sometimes have difficulty seeking help from a mentor or peer.	I often feel a sense of isolation in my work.
My work relationships are characterized by the free exchange of ideas.	My work relationships are dominated by the question of who is doing what for whom.	I have few or no close associates.
I am effective at different kinds of work in several different contexts.	For me, being productive requires "getting away from it all."	I seek out an isolated work environment.

Being a Shooting Star

At times of rapid change and advancement, leaders are at risk of becoming shooting stars, burning brightly and moving fast, then suddenly and unexpectedly crashing back to Earth. If your life centers entirely on your career and you are always on the go, traveling incessantly to get ahead, you are at risk of becoming a shooting star whose life is spiraling out of control.

The increasing pace of organizational life, fueled by information technology, globalization, and hypercompetition, creates a growing demand for talented people interested in being on the fast track. High achievement and top leadership posts often come to those who start early and run fast.

As an emerging leader, you may be at risk of becoming a shooting star just when you are moving up so rapidly in your career that you never have time to learn from your mistakes. When you move on after only a year or two in any job, and never stop to make an honest assessment of your leadership, you will never have to confront the results of your decisions. When you see problems of your own making coming back to haunt you, your response will probably be to become anxious rather than to summon the determination to apply the painful lessons of your experience.

Because your organization views you as a star, you have tempting levers to pull. For example, you can threaten your employer with a move to another organization if you are not promoted. If you do this often enough, one day you may find yourself in a high-level position where you are overwhelmed by an intractable set of problems. At this point, you will be prone to impulsive or even irrational decisions, because you have no grounding in your life that enables you to cope with these problems in a rational matter. This is the point when shooting stars flame out, come crashing down, and are forced to face their own reality.

When you feel the urgency to escape from your current dilemmas and move to a new position, this is the time to check on whether you are moving so fast that you have lost touch with your inner compass and are losing your bearings.

The Shooting Star

Leaders who fall into the shooting star trap lack the grounding of an integrated life. They rarely make time for family, friendships, their communities, or even themselves. Much-needed sleep and exercise are continually deferred. As they run ever faster, their stress mounts.

EXERCISE 2.5: IDENTIFYING THE SHOOTING STAR IN ME

This exercise focuses on identifying times in your life when you were at risk of becoming a shooting star.

Describe the run-up to a situation in which you were becoming a shooting star and what happened in that situation.

_____

_____

_____

What were the main feelings I had at the time?

_____

_____

_____

What did I do to recover?

_____

_____

_____

What would I do now to avoid the risk of burning out if I were confronted by a similar situation today?

_____

_____

_____

In Table 2.6, circle any of the characterizations that you identify with your present leadership.

If you circled examples in the Early Warning and Red Alert columns, you will want to pay particular attention to Chapter Eight, "Integrate Your Life," in Part Two.

GETTING BACK ON TRACK IS A SOURCE OF STRENGTH

In this chapter, you have begun to see how you, like all other leaders, can lose your way—can be pulled off the course of your True North by the pressures and seductions that you face. Being authentic as a leader is not about being perfect.

Table 2.6: Indicators of the Shooting Star in Me

Healthy Approaches to Wanting to Advance	*Early Warning Signs*	*Red Alerts*
I commit to achieving my goals.	To achieve my goals, I carve away other parts of my life, such as weekends or vacations.	I sometimes feel exhausted when working toward my goals.
I build my capacity through continuous learning.	I focus on finding opportunities to do what I already do best.	My best sometimes feels stale or old.
I look for the right position and level that match my capabilities and aspirations.	I look for new challenges before my current challenge has been met.	I have moved rapidly from job to job and assignment to assignment for a long time.
I bring out the best in others as I bring out the best in myself.	I focus on being seen at my best at all times.	I bring out my best even when it drives down others around me.
I am devoted to my work.	My work contributes to my losing contact with friends and puts strains on my family life.	I do not know my neighbors, my children's friends, or my partner.

It is much more about owning where you have gone off track and learning from your experience. You probably also have discovered that some of the hazards we have described—being an imposter, rationalizing, glory seeking, playing the loner, and being a shooting star—show up more often than the others in your self-evaluation. As challenging as this must be, you will find in the self-awareness chapter that knowing this truth will help accelerate your development as an authentic leader.

In the next chapter, "Leadership Development in the Crucible," you begin to discern the behaviors that will allow you to shift your orientation to each of the five hazards.

KEY TAKE-AWAYS

- All leaders are prone to losing their way at one point or another on their leadership journey.
- All leaders desire rewards and acceptance from others, and all desire to avoid negative consequences.
- The five hazards of leadership—being in impostor, rationalizer, glory seeker, loner, or shooting star—spring from these desires.
- Learning from his or her experiences with these hazards helps the individual along the path of becoming an authentic leader.

SUGGESTED READING

Finkelstein, S. *Why Smart Executives Fail and What You Can Learn from Their Mistakes*. New York: Portfolio, 2003.

Fiorina, C. *Tough Choices*. New York: Portfolio, 2006.

Goleman, D. *Destructive Emotions*. New York: Bantam Books, 2003.

Kohlreiser, G. *Hostage at the Table*. San Francisco: Jossey-Bass, 2006.

Maccoby, M. *The Productive Narcissist*. Los Angeles: Broadway Books, 2003.

3

Leadership Development in the Crucible

When heated directly by fire, the fire of trial, the heat of disease,
Infernos of grief and penury . . .
Can we hold under the terror, the torment of transforming, under forging,
Until we are bearers of light, torches, for sufferance, for illumining oblivion?
—*Susan Deborah King, from "Crucible," in* One-Breasted Woman

In this chapter, you will explore the crucible of your leadership—that time when you came face-to-face with yourself and recognized that life was about far more than being the hero of your own journey. By digging deeper into your life story, you will have the opportunity to focus on the crucial aspects that can help you unlock your development as a leader.

It can be hard to gain insight and learn from periods of productive ferment, difficulties, and challenges when you are in the midst of them. Yet it is during the most difficult times of your life that you have the opportunity to confront who you are at the deepest level and realize what your life—and your leadership—are about.

THE GREATEST CRUCIBLE OF YOUR LIFE

In their book *Geeks and Geezers*, Warren Bennis and Robert Thomas describe the crucible as an experience that tests leaders to their limits. A crucible can be triggered by such events as confronting a difficult situation at work, receiving critical feedback, or losing your job. Or it may result from a painful personal experience, such as divorce, illness, or the death of a loved one. "The skills required to conquer adversity and emerge stronger and more committed than ever," they conclude, "are the same ones that make for extraordinary leaders." The process of developing these skills is the focus of this guide. You can apply these skills at any time in your life.

> To a chemist, a crucible is a vessel in which substances are heated to high temperatures in order to trigger a chemical transformation, as in the case of the refinement of gold ore, or a steel refinery's blast furnace. The crucible is an ancient technology, and has yielded rich literary references over time, ranging from the refiner's fire of the Old Testament prophets, to the metaphor and techniques of alchemists, to Arthur Miller's play "The Crucible," about the Salem Witch Trials.

At some point in their lives, most people find themselves in a difficult situation or crucible. They may be undertaking new tasks, confronting new challenges, working at a new pace or with new degrees of responsibility—all with heightened stakes for success or failure.

As painful as these experiences may be, the resulting crucible may cause you to challenge your underlying assumptions about who you are, enable you to redefine your values, or help you see the major themes that weave an underlying thread throughout your life.

Have you ever found yourself in a situation where your life suddenly feels out of your control? As hard as you try to take control of your life at these times, in reality the events swirling about you are controlling you. You may be in denial about who you are trying to be in this situation, or you may be losing your way in the midst of the turmoil. You may be in a crucible and not even recognize it. But then things get so traumatic that you are forced to look at the person in the mirror and acknowledge your role in the drama taking place around you.

Your crucible tests you to the core of your being. It forces you to look at yourself, examine your character and your values in a new light, and come to grips with who you really are. Viewed in retrospect, your crucible may become the defining experience in your life, even if you do not recognize it when you are in the middle of the experience. Your crucible provides the opportunity for deep self-reflection that causes you to question your most basic assumptions and values, and your view of yourself in the world.

LEARNING FROM YOUR CRUCIBLE

Passing through the crucible—or reframing it years later with the benefit of hindsight—you will see the world differently, and thus you will behave differently as well. It is during such a passage that you recognize that your leadership is not primarily about your own success or about getting others to follow you. Rather, you understand that the essence of your leadership is aligning your teammates around a shared vision and shared values and empowering them to step up and lead. In *True North* we defined periods like these as the "transformation from 'I' to 'We.'"

Whereas success tends to reinforce your current behaviors, challenges force you to rethink your approach. By going through the often painful process of reliving and rethinking your earlier experience, you can see it through a different lens. Whereas before you may have viewed yourself as a victim of life's injustices, now you can find the power in having had those experiences and recognize that they give you the passion to use your leadership to help others.

For some leaders, the difficult experiences occurred at a young age, but a triggering event many years later caused them to reframe their experiences and find their calling to lead authentically. Figure 1.1, "The Journey to Authentic Leadership," in *True North* (page 16) shows the crucible as an integral part of your midcareer growth. However, it may be that events then only serve to trigger memories of earlier events in your life when you faced difficulties, and enable you to reframe them in terms of what you want your leadership to be.

As you read in the stories of Dan Vasella, Oprah Winfrey, and Marilyn Carlson Nelson in *True North*, a crucible may come at any time in life. For many people, their crucibles may not appear at first glance to be extreme in terms of loss, hardship, or challenge. But as they reflect on them, these early life experiences, such as significant family conflicts, challenges of maturation, or difficulties in their junior high or high school years, may leave imprints that stay with them through their adult years until they acknowledge and understand their impact on their lives.

EXERCISE 3.1: WRITING THE STORY OF MY CRUCIBLE

Write a letter to yourself that tells the story of your life's crucible. Write it in one continuous draft, allowing as much space as you need to complete the letter.

As you write, tell the whole story—setting the stage, narrating the high point and what changed, and surveying the consequences and aftereffects. As you write your story, listen to yourself as your friends would if they had access to relevant information about your experiences and the context around them.

The greatest crucible of my life is:

_____

_____

_____

_____

_____

_____

_____

_____

_____

_____

_____

_____

_____

_____

_____

_____

_____

_____

_____

Looking back at my letter,

The reasons why this experience was so challenging for me:

_____

_____

_____

The most stressful, challenging, or hard-to-endure time in my story was:

_____

_____

_____

I have been able to resolve the impact of my crucible experience on my life by:

_____

_____

_____

_____

Before you leave the story of your crucible, take a moment to examine yourself when you were in the midst of this situation as well as to observe your feelings right now.

What thoughts or feelings did I have as I worked on describing and understanding my crucible?

_____

_____

_____

What resources did I call upon to get through this crucible?

_____

_____

_____

What fundamental insights about who I am did I learn from my crucible?

_____

_____

_____

_____

THE TRANSFORMATION FROM "I" TO "WE"

We've all seen the traits in our bosses, subordinates, colleagues, and ourselves: they have the right skills, use the latest management tools, articulate the right messages with the most popular buzzwords, and hone the right strategies. But underneath something seems to be missing. Followers respond with caution. Supervisors are worried, but can't pin down what's wrong. Even concerned friends keep their distance. Even though all the pieces seem to be there, these leaders are never able to rally sustained support from their teams.

This is because these leaders have a predominantly "I" orientation.

Leaders often begin their careers with a primary focus on themselves—their performance, achievements, and rewards. As they enter the world of work, they envision themselves in the image of an all-conquering hero who can change the world for the better. The early years of leaders' lives are often spent in education, skills development, and initial leadership experiences.

You might think that the archetypal hero would be a natural model for an organization leader. We learned from our interviews with authentic leaders that the hero stage is a useful initial stage. Yet many leaders have difficulty in moving beyond it. As young leaders are promoted from individual roles to management, they may believe they are being recognized for their heroic abilities to produce results.

"We spend our early years trying to be the best," said Jaime Irick of General Electric. "To get into West Point or General Electric, you have to be the best. That is defined by what you can do on your own—your ability to be a phenomenal analyst or consultant or do well on a standardized test."

In spite of the rewards for heroic performance, authentic leaders reach a point on their journeys when their way forward is blocked or their worldview is turned upside down. They find that their journey is not following the straight ascending path depicted in Figure 1.1 in *True North*, but resembles the ups and downs traced around it. Successes are mirrored by challenges as the highs are followed by dips.

As leaders experience challenging times and learn the lessons of those difficult periods, the process of transforming from "I" to "We" is seeded. Initial success may reinforce what leaders do at an early stage, but difficult times force them to question their approach. At some point, authentic leaders begin to rethink what their life and leadership are all about. They may start to ask, "Do I have to do it all *myself*?" "Why can't I get this team to achieve the goals I have set forth?"

For some, the transformation to becoming an authentic leader results from the positive experience of having a wise mentor or having a unique opportunity at a young age. But as much as all of us want positive experiences like these, transformations for most leaders result from going through the difficult times in the crucible.

We single out the transformation from "I" to "We" because it places leaders in a powerful paradox. Recovering from a life-changing experience requires the continued deployment of the competitive drive and skills that leaders have been working to master to that point. At the same time, their experiences force them to be humble. This newly found humility stems from the recognition that leadership is not just about them.

Only when you stop focusing on your own ego will you be able to develop other leaders. You will be able to move beyond being competitive with talented peers and subordinates, and you will be more open to other points of view. As you overcome your need to control everything or do everything, you find that people are more interested in working with you. A light bulb goes on as you recognize the unlimited potential of empowered leaders working together toward a shared purpose. This transformation opens the door to discovering your full potential as an authentic leader.

As GE's Irick went on to say, "If you want to be a leader, you've got to flip that switch and understand that it's about serving the folks on your team. This is a very simple concept, but one that many people overlook. The sooner people realize it, the faster they will grow into leaders."

The transformation from "I" to "We" is the point of embarkation on the leader's journey. It propels the individual into the next stages of leadership development as the hero's journey is left behind and the leader's journey begins.

EXERCISE 3.2: HOW MY CRUCIBLE EXPERIENCE HELPS ME MOVE FROM "I" TO "WE"

This exercise focuses on understanding how your leadership crucible may transform your leadership and enable you to make the transition from "I" to "We."

How has my crucible experience enabled me to discover my passions for making a difference in the world?

_____

_____

_____

_____

How has my crucible affected my view of my leadership, and my ability to operate from a "We" orientation?

_____

_____

_____

_____

_____

_____

_____

_____

_____

_____

_____

_____

_____

_____

_____

_____

EXERCISE 3.3: WHERE AM I IN MOVING FROM "I" TO "WE"?

In reality, there are times when you are "I" oriented, and other times when you are "We" oriented. The important question is how much of your time as a leader is spent in one rather than the other, and whether you can lead from the orientation you need, when you need it. The purpose of this exercise is to learn where you are in shifting from an "I" orientation to a "We" orientation.

Looking at your life story, describe a time when you were leading from an "I" orientation.

_____

_____

_____

Describe a time when you were leading from a "We" orientation.

_____

_____

_____

_____

In leading from a "We" orientation, what impact did I have on others and on the results I wanted to achieve? How did this compare with the "I" orientation?

_____

_____

_____

_____

What percentage of my time is currently marked by leading from the "We" orientation? What percentage of my time should this be?

Leading from "We": At present _____%   In the future _____%

What action steps am I taking to lead more consistently from a "We" orientation?

1. _____

2. _____

3. _____

4. _____

5. _____

GUIDING YOUR LEADERSHIP DEVELOPMENT

In this chapter, you have begun to understand and befriend your crucible. This is the most important step you will take toward discovering your True North. The more detailed and specific your understanding of the story, the clearer your insights will be as you continue to work with this guide.

We also singled out the transformation from "I" to "We" that holds the key to your leadership. At this point in your work with this guide, you should understand better where you are in the process of that transformation and what role your crucible plays in it.

With this chapter we bring Part One, "Examine Your Leadership Journey," to a close. In Part Two, "Discover Your Authentic Leadership," you move to the specific steps you need to take to develop as an authentic leader.

KEY TAKE-AWAYS

- The greatest crucible of your life has a significant impact on learning about yourself and your life.

- Your crucible also shapes your passions to lead.

- Understanding your crucible can help you move from an "I" to a "We" orientation, which is critical for your development as an authentic leader.

SUGGESTED READING

Armstrong, L. *It's Not About the Bike*. New York: Penguin Putnam, 2002.

Bennis, W., and Thomas, R. *Geeks and Geezers*. Boston: Harvard Business School Press, 2002.

Campbell, J. *The Hero's Journey*. Novato, Calif.: New World Library, 1990.

Coelho, P. *The Alchemist*. New York: HarperCollins, 2006.

Kushner, H. *When Bad Things Happen to Good People*. New York: Hall, 1981.

Lansing, A. *Endurance: Shackleton's Incredible Voyage*. New York: Carroll & Graf, 1959.

Maslow, A. *Maslow on Management*. Hoboken, N.J.: Wiley, 1998.

Quinn, R. E. *Building the Bridge as You Walk on It: A Guide for Leading Change*. San Francisco: Jossey-Bass, 2004.

Read, P. P. *Alive: The Story of the Andes Survivors*. New York: Avon, 2002.

Smith, D. K. *On Value and Values: Thinking Differently About We in an Age of Me*. Upper Saddle River, N.J.: Prentice Hall, 2004.

Useem, M. *The Leadership Moment*. New York: Three Rivers Press, 1998.

Vasella, D. *Magic Cancer Bullet*. New York: Harper Business, 2003.

Part Two

Discover Your
Authentic Leadership

> Follow your compass and not your clock.
> —*Ann Moore, CEO, Time, Inc.*

In Part One, you went through a detailed self-assessment process that got you in touch with the story of your leadership journey. You learned about the pitfalls of losing your way, focused on your most challenging moments, examined your crucible experience, and studied the transformation from "I" to "We." Now you are ready to take on one of the greatest challenges of your life: discovering your authentic leadership by developing yourself.

In *True North* we addressed the challenges that all leaders face in staying aligned with their True North—their most deeply held beliefs, values, and principles—as they cope with the pressures and seductions of leading in the real world. To do that, you will need a compass to guide you on your journey.

Refer to the compass diagram in *True North* (page xxxv). The compass provides you with the basics you need to develop yourself. They include:

47

At the center of your compass: Build Your Self-Awareness
To the north: Live Your Values
To the east: Use Your Motivated Capabilities
To the south: Build Your Support Team
To the west: Lead an Integrated Life

Each of these areas takes development and hard work on your part. There are no shortcuts here, no quick fixes, no "becoming an authentic leader in seven easy steps." To become an authentic leader, first you must take responsibility for your own development and then use this compass to guide your process. Part Two consists of five chapters, each focused on a specific element of your authentic leadership development. We derived these five areas—self-awareness, practicing your values, using your motivated capabilities, building your support team, and leading an integrated life—from our interviews with the leaders who told us about the ways in which they developed themselves as authentic leaders.

As you go through the process and exercises outlined in Part Two, you will find that the pieces all fit together as an integrated whole. Taken together, they enable you to stay focused on your True North while coping with and overcoming the greatest challenges you will be confronted with as a leader.

You are embarking on an exciting journey as you discover your authentic leadership. Let's get started.

Chapter 4　Build Your Self-Awareness
Chapter 5　Live Your Values
Chapter 6　Find the Sweet Spot of Your Motivated Capabilities
Chapter 7　Build Your Support Team
Chapter 8　Integrate Your Life

4

Build Your Self-Awareness

It was as if someone flashed a mirror at me at my absolute worst.
What I saw was horrifying, but it was also a great lesson.
—Doug Baker Jr., chairman and CEO, Ecolab

We have placed self-awareness at the center of the True North compass because it is key to knowing and following your True North. A compass needle orients itself to Earth's magnetic field. To do so, it pivots on the fixed point of a tiny fulcrum. Your self-awareness is the pivot on which your balanced development depends. Without self-awareness, your orientation to your True North can never be sure.

This chapter is aimed at providing the tools to build your self-awareness. It will help you know when something is authentic for you and when it is not. The goal of this chapter is to identify times when others have helped you gain self-awareness and also times when you missed opportunities. From this knowledge, you can build your own toolkit for increasing your self-awareness, and with it the capacity to accept and regulate yourself.

These exercises start with taking stock of how you view yourself. Because it is impossible to be truly self-aware without honest and direct feedback from others, we recommend that you enlist the assistance of trusted peers, mentors, and friends. You will have the opportunity to reflect on this feedback and explore what changes it suggests in your approach to life and leadership.

SELF-AWARENESS CAN BE DEVELOPED

In the ten years since Daniel Goleman wrote his groundbreaking book, *Emotional Intelligence*, EQ has become of equal importance to IQ as an essential quality for leaders, especially those with broad leadership responsibilities. The exercise that follows will help you think about the ways you can gain self-awareness and improve your emotional intelligence.

EXERCISE 4.1: ASSESSING MY SELF-AWARENESS

The following questions will allow you to compare your evaluation of yourself with how others view you. For those questions asking for a numerical evaluation, rate yourself on a 1–5 scale (with 1 meaning to the least extent or degree, 3 meaning to a moderate extent or degree, and 5 meaning to the greatest extent or degree), then support your assessment by answering each question.

Next, choose at least five people who know you well to rate you using the same scale and to provide their assessments. (For additional forms, visit www .truenorthleaders.com or www.authleadership.com.) The more people you pick, the more complete the feedback you will receive. Their feedback will be more accurate if you allow them to remain anonymous.

I. Self-Awareness

Self-awareness: the ability to recognize and understand your moods, emotions, and drives as well as your effect on others.

	Self-Rating (1–5)	Rating from Others (1–5)
How self-confident am I?		
How aware am I of my moods, my emotions, and my drives?		
How effective am I in recognizing my effect on other people?		

Describe a situation in which you demonstrated a lack of self-awareness.

_____

_____

_____

_____

_____

What steps should I take to improve my self-awareness?

1. _____

2. _____

3. _____

4. _____

5. _____

Overall assessment of my self-awareness (1–5): _____ _____
                                                      (self)   *(others)*

II. Self-Regulation

Self-regulation: the ability to control or redirect disruptive impulses and moods; the ability to think before acting and to suspend judgment.

	Self-Rating (1–5)	Rating from Others (1–5)
How effective am I in regulating my moods so as to minimize their impact on other people?		
To what extent am I able to suspend judgment of others and their ideas, in order to gain a full understanding first?		
When confronted with situations that are displeasing to me, to what extent am I able to take the time to think clearly about them before responding or reacting?		
When I receive critical feedback from others, how well am I able to take in the feedback and respond in a constructive manner without acting defensively or attacking the provider of the feedback?		
To what extent am I comfortable with ambiguity and change?		

Describe a situation in which you demonstrated a lack of self-regulation.

_____

_____

_____

_____

What steps should I take to improve my self-regulation?

1. _____

2. _____

3. _____

4. _____

5. _____

Overall assessment of my self-regulation (1–5): _____   _____

(self)   (others)

III. Empathy

Empathy: the ability to understand the emotional makeup of other people and to be sensitive to their emotional needs.

	Self-Rating (1–5)	Rating from Others (1–5)
How well do I understand the emotional makeup of others and their needs?		
How sensitive am I in relating to their needs and helping them?		
To what extent do I get feedback from others that I have empathy?		

Describe a situation in which you demonstrated a lack of empathy for others.

_____

_____

_____

_____

_____

What steps should I take to be more empathic?

1. _____

2. _____

3. _____

4. _____

5. _____

Overall assessment of my empathy (1–5): _____ _____

(self)   *(others)*

One of the hardest things for all of us is to see ourselves as others see us. When you review your feedback, you may find that your self-assessment differs from the assessments you receive from others. These discrepancies represent areas that are worth further exploration on your part. How and why does your perspective differ from that of others? The path of authentic leadership development lies in this exploration, not in having all the answers line up perfectly.

DISCOVERING YOUR AUTHENTIC SELF

It is impossible to be authentic without being aware of your core strengths, your weaknesses, and your underdeveloped areas. You also need to develop an understanding of your blind spots, areas of resilience, and vulnerabilities.

We all know people who represent themselves in one way and then behave in exactly the opposite manner. In reality, you may have been guilty of this as well. This is a working definition of being inauthentic. Authenticity is not about being perfect, either. People who behave as if they are perfect are just as inauthentic.

As we have seen from our research, those leaders who can speak openly about their weaknesses, blind spots, and vulnerabilities permit others to do the same. If you can do this, you will create deep levels of trust and commitment in your relationships. Thus you will be living with the humble truth of owning and accepting all of who you are, both the gifts and the challenges.

We each have many aspects that we present to the world in layered succession. In *True North*, we introduced the metaphor of the onion with all its layers.

(See Figure 4.1, "Peeling Back the Onion," page 77 of *True North*.) Outer layers are expressions of our external identity to the world. These are the first signals to other people about who we are and what lies beneath. Yet they are also forms of protection; they prevent the world from intruding on our core selves. Underneath the outer layer are deeper layers: our strengths and weaknesses, our needs and desires. These are the elements from which we operate in the world. Deeper still lie our values and motivations, the criteria that define our own sense of success and fulfillment in the world.

Most hidden of all are our shadow sides, our vulnerabilities, and our blind spots. We all have them, whether or not we are aware of them or willing to acknowledge them. Oftentimes others see these aspects of our being, even if we do not. These areas are labeled as our "blind spots." These deeper layers contribute directly to our authenticity as leaders, yet by their nature they are difficult to identify unless we are brutally honest with ourselves or invite others to give us feedback about such vulnerable places.

At the core of our being lies our authentic self—our true and genuine nature. If we can "own" all aspects of who we are, we can live in harmony with our authentic selves and present our true self to others and to the world around us. Our True North comes from this authentic place, from which we find our calling to leadership.

Why is the outer skin of our onion so tough? For fear of being judged harshly by others, or even being rejected by them, we are understandably reluctant to expose our deeper layers. We want to display our strengths, but are reluctant to expose our weaknesses. We want to state our desires, but naturally we are concerned about the power others gain over us when they see our needs. Deeper down, our values and motivations are important sources of authentic leadership.

As a result of our fears, we often try to cover up the core where our vulnerabilities, weaknesses, blind spots, and shadow sides reside. Many of us are so good at covering them up that we ourselves are not aware of them, yet others quickly observe them. We may be in denial about their existence until we are forced into situations where they are exposed. In leadership, being forced into a situation where parts of ourselves are suddenly exposed can lead to losing our way.

The paradox underlying this process of showing only parts of ourselves while hiding others is that our vulnerabilities, shadow sides, and blind spots are also the parts of us most starved for expression, acceptance, and integration. When we do not acknowledge them as being just as critical to who we are as our strengths, they cause us to behave in inauthentic ways. Only when we embrace these aspects of ourselves can we become fully authentic as human beings.

SELF-ACCEPTANCE

The good news about self-awareness is that it can lead you to accept yourself as you really are. It is a simple fact that none of us can be the best at everything. Each of us has a set of strengths that come naturally, talents we have developed over time, and things we are never going to be good at. At the same time, what enables us to be authentic and effective leaders is maximizing the use of our strengths—not focusing on our weaknesses—and surrounding ourselves with others whose strengths complement our own and fill in for our gaps. The ability to accept yourself as you are is a gift that leads not only to self-acceptance but to true freedom.

We have found that accepting yourself for who you are and loving yourself unconditionally require compassion for yourself. For you to acknowledge your weaknesses and shadow sides, you will have to accept the things you like least about yourself as integral to who you are. We see this illustrated in Bill's experience in learning to accept his weaknesses:

> *In 1997 when I was chairman and CEO of Medtronic, I was driving from down-town Minneapolis to my office listening to a CD featuring an address by poet David Whyte called "The Poetry of Self-Compassion." One of the poems recited by Whyte was "Love After Love" [see sidebar], by the Nobel Prize–winning poet Derek Walcott. Walcott's poem talks about the challenge of getting in touch with those parts of ourselves that we have rejected, denied, and ignored for many years. Walcott encourages us to "invite them in to the feast that is our life."*

> *I was so stunned by these words as I listened to Whyte recite the poem that I pulled my car over to the shoulder of I-94 several times in order to write them down. In retrospect, this seems pretty silly, as this was just a CD, and I could have easily written down the poem after I arrived at my office.*

Love After Love

Derek Walcott

The time will come when, with elation,
You will greet yourself, arriving at your own door,
In your own mirror, and each will smile at the other's welcome,
And say, sit here. Eat.
You will love again the stranger who was yourself.
Give wine. Give bread. Give back your heart to itself,
To the stranger who has loved you all your life,
Whom you ignored for another,
Who knows you by heart.
Take down the love letters from the bookshelf,
The photographs, the desperate notes,
Peel your own image from the mirror.
Sit. Feast on your life.

Why was I so stunned by these words? I was moved because I had been trying so hard to be perfect all my life that I had rejected my shadow sides and my vulnerabilities for more than forty years. In that moment I finally recognized that I had been rejecting parts of myself that I did not like and had tried unsuccessfully to hide from others. These included my impatience, direct manner of challenging others, and often aggressive behavior, coupled with a long ago memory of being a skinny kid who was picked on by bigger kids in junior high. Even worse, I had been blaming these characteristics on my then-deceased father, who had similar traits, instead of accepting them as integral to who I am. This poem finally enabled me to accept myself with all my warts. Once I did so, I found I could love all of myself, not just the good parts, and become much more authentic in my relationships with others. Even more important, accepting myself for who I was, flaws and all, became very liberating for me.

EXERCISE 4.2: PEELING BACK THE ONION

The purpose of this exercise is to help you become aware of your underdeveloped areas.

What are some areas where I feel vulnerable to exposure?

1. _____
2. _____
3. _____
4. _____
5. _____

What are my shadow sides, those aspects of my being that I do not like to acknowledge?

1. _____
2. _____
3. _____
4. _____
5. _____

Many leaders find that their strengths are related to their vulnerabilities and shadow sides. Although specific elements of your makeup may be hard to accept, when you see them as an integral part of who you are, just as you see the elements of which you are most proud, you may find that it is easier to accept yourself with all your strengths and weaknesses. You will likely also find that it becomes easier to develop yourself as an authentic leader.

THE LESSONS OF FEEDBACK

Feedback can be one of the most valuable ways of gaining greater self-awareness and developing the capacity to see yourself as others see you. It is only through others that you see your blind spots.

EXERCISE 4.3: GETTING HONEST
FEEDBACK FROM OTHERS

The purpose of this exercise is to practice getting honest feedback from others so that you can learn from it. For many leaders, the experience of getting feedback is often rare, or it is combined with being evaluated for performance, compensation, or promotion purposes. Under those conditions, it is very hard to learn about yourself.

Describe a situation in which you received useful feedback from someone else or a group of people.

_____

_____

_____

_____

_____

How did I react to the feedback? What were my feelings about it and the person who gave it?

_____

_____

_____

List the ways in which you were able to change your behavior in response to the feedback.

_____

_____

_____

_____

Are you prepared to share your perceived strengths, weaknesses, vulnerabilities, and shadow sides with someone to whom you feel very close? If so, we suggest that you seek them out for feedback at your earliest opportunity. Solicit their feedback on how they perceive you. Record your thoughts below.

The perceptions of someone close to me were the same as mine and different from mine in the following ways:

_____

_____

_____

_____

_____

LEARNING FROM DIFFICULT FEEDBACK

Good friends tell you when you're behaving in inauthentic ways. With the right team around you, you can benefit from information about your blind spots and address them directly.

Blind spots are areas that are visible to others but not to yourself. Like the area in the rear-view mirror of your automobile where you cannot see the car in the lane next to you, blind spots in your self-awareness can easily be overlooked because you are completely unaware of their presence. You don't even know they are there—you don't know what you don't know about yourself.

This is where you need the help of others—not your critics, but people you trust who will hold up a mirror to your face that helps you recognize your blind spots. The trick is to take the person in that mirror seriously and work on recognizing your blind spots. Practice checking on them from time to time to see if you can recognize them.

EXERCISE 4.4: GETTING FEEDBACK ON MY BLIND SPOTS

The purpose of this exercise is to get feedback from someone close to you about your blind spots. Prepare for this exercise by rereading the story of Doug Baker's experience of getting feedback from his subordinates (page 53 of *True North*). He says the experience felt as if "someone flashed a mirror at me at my absolute worst."

Now consider the feedback you received from others in Exercise 4.1, or ask someone close to you to describe what he or she perceives to be your blind spots.

What did I learn about myself from the other person's feedback?

1. _____

2. _____

3. _____

4. _____

5. _____

LEARNING ABOUT YOURSELF IS AN ONGOING PROCESS

In our research, we learned that authentic leaders are always asking for honest feedback from others in order to calibrate their view of themselves. To incorporate that feedback into their behaviors, they then develop regular practices for reflection and introspection. We heard from many of our interviewees for *True North* that journaling, meditation, spiritual work and religious practice, and individual physical exercise—all practices associated with reflection and introspection—were widely used for gaining deeper self-awareness.

Some find that meditation is a valuable way to clear their minds and reflect on what is important to them. For those with regular religious practices, prayer can be a very meaningful means of reflecting and being introspective. For others, physical exercise, such as jogging or brisk walking by themselves, provides the opportunity for being introspective and understanding themselves better. Finally, some prefer to discuss personal issues with their significant other, best friend, mentor, coach, or therapist.

There are two keys to making these practices effective in gaining self-awareness and self-acceptance. The first is to be completely open with yourself as well as with at least one other person in your life. The second is to develop regular habits and times to be introspective. You should work these practices into your daily life, not just look at them as a one-time exercise.

Because there is no secret to self-awareness that lies outside yourself, any pathway that reveals your true self to you can bear fruit. Being curious about your inner self and pushing back the boundaries of your inner awareness through reflection and introspection are the best paths toward self-awareness.

As important as this introspective work is, we have found that for many people, developing their authentic leadership is accomplished in relationships with other people. Because leading is about relationships, you can enhance your reflection and introspection in service of deepening your authentic leadership by using the support of people with whom you feel enough trust to open yourself up.

The goal of self-awareness is self-knowledge, and ultimately self-acceptance—self-acceptance as the leader you are as well as the leader you are capable of becoming.

EXERCISE 4.5: TAKE-AWAYS ON SELF-AWARENESS AND SELF-ACCEPTANCE

The purpose of this exercise is to gather together the insights you have gained and the further questions you have, now that you are completing this chapter.

Based on the feedback I received, what are my greatest needs for development as a leader?

1. _____

2. _____

3. _____

4. _____

5. _____

What are some ways I can become more self-aware?

1. _____
2. _____
3. _____
4. _____
5. _____

What are the ways I will try to improve my self-acceptance?

1. _____
2. _____
3. _____
4. _____
5. _____

SELF-AWARENESS IS PREPARATION FOR GROWTH

In this chapter, you have begun to see how others see you and, most important, begun to understand your blind spots. You looked at the many layers of the onion, not just the skin. Once you see how all the layers are necessary and how they make up a whole, you can begin to be more self-accepting. Following your True North is a journey that requires you to see clearly the territory you are passing through if you are to stay on track.

In the next chapter, we move to uncover your core leadership values. They can help you find your True North.

KEY TAKE-AWAYS

- Not being aware of how others see you can cause you to behave inauthentically.
- Self-awareness is necessary in order for you to find and follow your True North.

- Your self has several layers, like an onion. The outer skin protects you, but it also keeps you from showing your authentic self and does not actually fool anyone but yourself.
- You can build self-awareness with direct and honest feedback from others.
- After you get critical feedback, it is important to process it through a period of reflection and introspection.
- Self-awareness is the key to improving your self-acceptance.

SUGGESTED READING

Bennis, W., and Tichy, N. *Judgment*. New York: Portfolio, 2007.

Cashman, K. *Leadership from the Inside Out*. Provo, Utah: Executive Excellence, 1998.

Conley, C. *Peak*. San Francisco: Jossey-Bass, 2007.

Gardner, H. *Intelligence Reframed*. New York: Basic Books, 1999.

Gladwell, M. *Blink*. New York: Little, Brown, 2000.

Goldsmith, M. *What Got You Here Won't Get You There*. New York: Hyperion, 2007.

Goleman, D. *Emotional Intelligence*. New York: Bantam Books, 1995.

Goleman, D., Boyatzis, R., and McKee, A. *Primal Leadership*. Boston: Harvard Business School Press, 2002.

Jaworski, J. *Synchronicity*. San Francisco: Berrett-Koehler, 1996.

Krishnamurti, J. *Total Freedom: The Essential Krishnamurti*. San Francisco: HarperSanFrancisco, 1996.

Maxwell, J. *Developing the Leader Within You*. London: Nelson, 2005.

Oliver, M. *New and Selected Poems*. Boston: Beacon Press, 1992.

Walcott, D. "Love After Love." In *Sea Grapes*. New York: Farrar, Straus & Giroux, 1976.

5

Live Your Values

> The softest pillow is a clear conscience.
> —*Narayana Murthy, founder and former CEO, Infosys*

It is important to be clear about your authentic values, leadership principles, and ethical boundaries so that you can put them into practice when leading. Living your values enables you to make sound leadership decisions and, more important, enables others to know who you are as a leader. In looking critically at your actions under pressure, you will learn from times when you lived by your values, and from those times when you deviated from them.

The exercises start with identifying your authentic leadership values. Next you will translate those values into their associated leadership principles. Last, you will define the ethical boundaries beyond which you will not go. By the end of the chapter, you should have a clear sense of your leadership values, principles, and ethical boundaries.

VALUES ARE PERSONAL

Leaders are defined by their values and their character. Practicing your values in a consistent way brings meaning to your work and life, and enables your life to be congruent and authentic. People trust their leaders when their leaders are predictable and give clear indications of what they will do when the chips are down.

When you lead, your actions are being watched, as you demonstrate your values in what you do. People around you are looking not only at the effectiveness of your actions but also at the way you act and the choices you make. Securing and

maintaining trust, and restoring it when it is strained, are among the most difficult and important challenges that leaders face.

Although fundamental values held by leaders are personal to themselves,
integrity is the one value that is required in every authentic leader. If you don't
exercise complete integrity in your leadership, no one can trust you. If other people cannot trust you, why would they want to work with you?

IDENTIFYING VALUES, PRINCIPLES, AND ETHICAL BOUNDARIES

To operate from your True North, you will need not only to know your values but
also to translate them into action. Those who develop a sense of their values,
principles, and ethical boundaries before they find themselves in the midst of a
crisis are better prepared to navigate through difficult decisions and dilemmas
when the pressure is on.

EXERCISE 5.1: IDENTIFYING MY VALUES

Values: the things that matter in your life.

The purpose of this exercise is to identify the set of values that you follow in
your leadership. In preparation for this exercise, review the path of life exercise
(Exercise 1.1). This exercise has three parts that prompt you to identify your values through several paths.

Part I. Building My List of Values

Work through the following list, quickly putting check marks next to any values
that should be on your list of core leadership values. As you do this, watch out for
picking up values that are desirable and noble, but are not values you express in
your leadership.

My Values

☐ Self-sufficiency ☐ Compassion ☐ Learning ☐ Teamwork
☐ Fun ☐ Inclusiveness ☐ Humility ☐ Authority
☐ Fulfillment ☐ Individuality ☐ Wealth ☐ Creativity
☐ Honor ☐ Fair play ☐ Happiness ☐ Achievement
☐ Faithfulness ☐ Freedom ☐ Edge ☐ Security
☐ Duty ☐ Ambition ☐ Change ☐ Openness
☐ Practicality ☐ Influence ☐ Responsibility ☐ Objectivity

Part II. My Most Important Values

Values come to life in your leadership. Now tighten up the list you created in Part I by listing only the values that are *most* important to your life and your leadership. The following are the most important values in my leadership:

1. _____   4. _____   7. _____   10. _____
2. _____   5. _____   8. _____   11. _____
3. _____   6. _____   9. _____   12. _____

Part III. Values in My Crucible

Return to Exercise 3.1, "Writing the Story of My Crucible," and ask yourself these questions about your leadership.

What values did I ignore when I was in the crucible?

1. _____

2. _____

3. _____

4. _____

5. _____

What were the values that got me through my crucible?

1. _____

2. _____

3. _____

4. _____

5. _____

Part IV. Clarifying My Definitions of My Values

Return to the lists in Parts I and II of this exercise and put check marks next to the values that must be on your list at all times. These may be difficult choices.

Next, list these values in Table 5.1 and write your own definition of what each value means for you. After you have listed them, go back and rank-order them by their importance to you.

Here are some examples of value definitions:

Integrity: tell the whole truth to others and operate within the law in all business concerns.

Learning: always be open to new ways of working, no matter how well the current model is working.

Table 5.1: My Definitions of My Values

Value Name	Value Definition	Rank

Which of your values are the most essential to you as an authentic leader, and are therefore inviolate? Which ones are desirable but not essential? Put an asterisk next to the values that are inviolate for you.

Part V. Translating My Values into Practice

Most leaders think they have good values. When things are going well, it is relatively easy to practice one's principles in a consistent manner. The real test comes when things are not going your way or when you can see years of success going up in flames. What will you do then? Everyone watches you to see what you will do under that pressure, when you are feeling the heat in the crucible. Will you deviate—just a little bit—in order to get through this crisis, thinking that you will return to your values when the crisis passes? If you do, others around you will no longer see you as someone who "walks the talk." Observing your example, others may assume that they too can deviate from their values under pressure.

For you, the situation is even more serious. Even though you may go back to practicing your values when the pressure eases, the next time you find yourself in a similar situation, you are likely to deviate again—especially if you got through it the first time without getting caught or being called to account for your behavior.

An even more critical test is what you will do when no one else is looking. We find that this is precisely the way that many leaders get in trouble: they think they won't get caught.

Can I look myself in the mirror and say that I have stayed true to my values under challenging circumstances? Or would I admit to myself that I have not?

_____

_____

_____

Looking back over your life story, describe a situation in which you deviated from your values in order to achieve your goals.

_____

_____

_____

_____

How will I handle this situation if I face it in the future?

_____

_____

_____

Many people get on a slippery slope with regard to their values, as minor deviations lead to major ones later on.

How can I sense when I am getting on this slippery slope?

_____

_____

_____

Part VI. Exploring Conflicts Among My Values

Looking back over your life story once again, describe a personal situation in which your values conflicted with each other.

_____

_____

_____

_____

_____

How did I resolve this conflict?

_____

_____

_____

Was I pleased with the outcome? How might I handle it differently in the future?

_____

_____

_____

Part VII. Testing My Values Under Pressure

Call to mind a situation in which your values were tested under pressure.

What resources did I call upon under this pressure?

_____

_____

_____

To what extent did I deviate from my values?

_____

_____

_____

What would I do differently if I had it do all over again?

_____

_____

_____

In this exercise, you explored how you have worked with the challenges of resolving conflicts among your values and of holding to your values under pressure. For every leader, values are tested in these ways all the time. The next part of this chapter will help you put your values into action through your leadership principles.

LEADERSHIP PRINCIPLES

The missing step in most values exercises is making your values actionable. Chances are that you have participated in at least one program or group session defining your values and those of your organization. In too many cases, these lists of values remain on the flip chart or in your notebook, because there is no focus on practicing your values. Putting values into practice is crucial for authentic leaders because, under pressure—in the loneliness of leadership—the only values you can count on are those that you have already tested and proven during your life.

Your leadership principles are an outgrowth of your values; they are the linchpin that links your values to the True North of your leadership.

EXERCISE 5.2: IDENTIFYING MY LEADERSHIP PRINCIPLES

Leadership principles: values translated into working practices, templates for behavior that clarify how you will lead in your work environment.

The purpose of this exercise is to translate your leadership values into leadership principles. Take each value and definition you created in Exercise 5.1 and turn them into concrete and visible leadership principles. What actions will you take to support that value?

Here is an example of a value definition translated into a leadership principle:

Integrity: tell the whole truth to others and operate within the law in all business concerns.

Integrity: in order to create a workplace environment that supports telling the whole truth one-on-one and in meetings, I will model that behavior myself.

Use Table 5.2 to record the leadership principles you will use in leading others. Once you have done the translation work, rate yourself on how well you

Table 5.2: My Leadership Principles

Value Name	Leadership Principle	Rating
	I will . . .	

are putting those principles into practice at the present time, using a 1–5 scale (1 = I'm failing to put this principle into practice; 3 = I'm doing an average job; 5 = I'm doing an excellent job of putting this principle into practice).

What has been hard for me in putting those principles into practice?

_____

_____

_____

What steps can I take tomorrow to put my leadership principles into practice?

_____

_____

_____

ESTABLISHING ETHICAL BOUNDARIES

Explicit ethical boundaries are the final line of defense against losing your True North. Whereas there may be times when you face conflicts among your values that force you to choose one over another, or when you cannot put your leadership principles into practice, your ethical boundaries represent the clear line in the sand that you will not cross, no matter what.

For example, in Bill's work at Medtronic, the practice of taking a physician out to dinner, going to a ball game, or having an educational meeting at an attractive resort might fall into the "gray area" of values, yet still be considered ethical. In contrast, giving any cash gift or gratuity to a customer anywhere in the world would violate his ethical boundaries and those of the company. Deviations from this boundary would be cause for immediate dismissal of an employee, no matter how valuable that person might be to the organization.

Some leaders have shared with us the practice of writing down their ethical boundaries on a small card that they then carry in their purse, wallet, briefcase, or carry-on. Once you have made such a list, it is a valuable exercise to review it periodically and give yourself a frank self-assessment about whether those boundaries are being tested—are their limits being stretched?—and whether the boundaries are sufficient.

Without such clear ethical boundaries, leaders may find that small deviations early on lead to larger ones later, especially if the earlier deviations are not detected. At this point leaders may discover that they are far outside their ethical standards with no way to get back inside. Unless they have the courage to admit to these ethical deviations, leaders may attempt to cover them up. That cover-up often leads to far greater consequences than the ethical deviation itself.

Much preferred is for leaders to establish their clear ethical boundaries before those boundaries are tested under the pressures and seductions of the real world.

EXERCISE 5.3: IDENTIFYING MY ETHICAL BOUNDARIES

Ethical boundaries: the limits placed on your actions, based on your standards of ethical behavior.

The purpose of this exercise is to identify and define ethical boundaries for your leadership.

The following are my ethical boundaries:

I will not . . .

1. _____
2. _____
3. _____
4. _____
5. _____
6. _____
7. _____
8. _____

Looking at your life story, describe a situation in which your ethical boundaries were tested.

_____

_____

_____

_____

_____

How did I respond?

_____

_____

_____

What will I do differently if I am confronted with a similar situation in the future?

_____

_____

_____

The Newspaper Test of Your Ethical Boundaries

Imagine that a challenging action from your work or home life that you are about to take will be published above the fold on the front page of your newspaper. Would you be proud or ashamed to have your colleagues, family, and friends read about it in stark black and white?

Close your eyes and listen to your intuition.

Imagine telling your partner, your parents, or your child about your decision and actions.

Take a deep breath and get in touch with the sensations of your body and its surroundings.

What is the "right" thing for me to do in this situation?

_____

_____

_____

_____

_____

(If your answer is that you would not be proud to have that article published, perhaps you should reexamine your behavior and look for ways that you can modify it.)

VALUES, PRINCIPLES, AND ETHICAL BOUNDARIES BENEFIT FROM PRACTICE

In this chapter, you clarified your core values as an authentic leader. You did this by integrating the values to which you aspire with those revealed through the lens of your leadership. In order to follow your True North, you need clear indicators that tell you when you are on track and when you are not. Through the process of defining your leadership principles, you began to see what it takes to live your values every day. Finally, looking at your ethical boundaries requires that you become attuned to the shades of gray that can sometimes obscure your vision. From here, we move on to clarifying the motivations that rest on your values.

KEY TAKE-AWAYS

- Your values are unique to you.
- You may not know what your real values are until they are tested under pressure.
- Dealing with situations where your values conflict reveals to you which values are most important to you.

- Your leadership principles define the way in which you apply your values every day.
- Establishing your ethical boundaries in advance will give you clarity about what to do when you are pushed to the limits.

SUGGESTED READING

Gergen, D. *Eyewitness to Power*. New York: Simon & Schuster, 2000.

Heifetz, R. *Leadership Without Easy Answers*. Cambridge, Mass.: Belknap, 1994.

Jansen, J. *I Don't Know What I Want, but I Know It's Not This: A Step-by-Step Guide to Finding Gratifying Work*. New York: Penguin, 2003.

Kabat-Zinn, J. *Wherever You Go, There You Are*. New York: Hyperion, 1994.

Payne, L. *Value Shift*. New York: McGraw-Hill, 2003.

Piper, T., Gentile, M., and Daloz-Parks, S. *Can Ethics Be Taught?* Boston: Harvard Business School Press, 1993.

6

Find the Sweet Spot of Your Motivated Capabilities

When you find a role that meshes your motivations with
your capabilities, you will discover the sweet spot
that maximizes your effectiveness as a leader.

There are times when your unique capabilities and your core motivations are completely synchronized. You are good at what you are doing, and you are on fire about doing it. You feel as if you are completely in the groove. When you find yourself in this position, you have discovered your sweet spot—that point where you are the most alive, most satisfied, and most closely aligned with your True North.

Although we all know what these times are like, they can be hard to find. In Chapter Six of *True North*, Charles Schwab relates that he tried several paths to develop his skills and make his way in the world. He tried and abandoned the law before turning to investment research. Despite his many efforts, his resilience and persistence did not pay off until he found work that both capitalized on his strength in math and satisfied his drive toward independence, financial success, and equal opportunity.

This is one of the promises of *True North*: when you are clear about your strengths and what you love, and when you express them consistently in your leadership, you will be a more effective leader. The things that usually wear you down get easier because they are mere stepping-stones to being able to utilize your motivated capabilities. Even more important, you will recognize opportunities to do what you love, and you will know how to create those opportunities for yourself.

Effective leadership is easier in situations that both motivate you and utilize your capabilities. Certainly, there are times when one has to be happy with only strong motivation or only great skill in any particular job or task. But ultimately you should put yourself in a place where you can enjoy both.

The key to your effectiveness as a leader will be to find positions that use your strongest capabilities and that are highly motivating to you. We label such positions your "sweet spot."

The work in this chapter begins with your motivation to lead.

EXERCISE 6.1: MY MOTIVATION TO LEAD

Motivation: the desires that cause people to pursue goals with energy and persistence.

Look at your life story and list the desires that have energized you as a leader.

My motivations to lead and to develop as a leader are:

1. _____
2. _____
3. _____
4. _____
5. _____
6. _____
7. _____
8. _____

Think through the source of each motivation listed above.

Where does the motivation come from in my life story?

1. _____
2. _____
3. _____
4. _____
5. _____
6. _____
7. _____
8. _____

DISCOVER YOUR INTRINSIC AND EXTRINSIC MOTIVATIONS

Sometimes your motivations are clear and predictable. At other times, you are motivated by deeper forces. To understand your motivations at a deeper level, you will examine two different categories of motivations: intrinsic and extrinsic.

Intrinsic motivations: motivations that have their origins within you, and are aligned with your True North.

Extrinsic motivations: motivations that have their origins in the external world.

The terms *intrinsic* and *extrinsic* literally mean "from within" and "from without." Extrinsic motivators include such things as monetary compensation, power, recognition, status, prestigious associations, and other carrots that motivate leaders. Extrinsic motivations are not problematic in themselves. Making money, holding power, and enjoying status and influence can be good things and bring joy to your life. What is wrong, then, about relying entirely on extrinsic motivations?

All of us are well trained, particularly in the business world, to respond to extrinsic motivations. Yet we may find that in spite of having our material needs fulfilled, we have a nagging feeling that our work lacks meaning. It is our intrinsic motivations that give a deeper sense of meaning and purpose to our lives.

Our research yielded a rich trove of intrinsic motivations. They included seeking personal growth and development and the satisfaction of doing a good job, providing for and helping others, leading and organizing others, creating a worthwhile product or service, finding meaning in one's efforts, being true to one's beliefs, making a difference in the world, and mentoring and having a positive influence on others.

Leaders gain insight into their intrinsic motivations during stressful and challenging times, on vacation, or during transitions between assignments. These are all times when we become more introspective.

EXERCISE 6.2: MY EXTRINSIC MOTIVATIONS

The purpose of this exercise and the one that follows is to guide you in identifying the motivations you have experienced in your life that give you energy and persistence, and in classifying them by whether they are intrinsic and extrinsic motivations.

What are your extrinsic motivations? Please fill in Table 6.1 with a specific expression of each category of extrinsic motivation you identify in your life story. For example, in the monetary compensation category, you might say, "Compensation in the top quartile of my peers."

After you have completed the list, rank-order your extrinsic motivations (1 being the most powerful).

Table 6.1: My Extrinsic Motivations

Category	My Extrinsic Motivations	Rank
1. Monetary compensation		
2. Having power		
3. Having a title		
4. Public recognition		
5. Social status		
6. Winning over others		
7. Association with prestigious institutions		
8. Other		

EXERCISE 6.3: MY INTRINSIC MOTIVATIONS

What are your intrinsic motivations? Please fill in Table 6.2 with a specific expression of each category of intrinsic motivation you identify in your story. For example, in the personal growth and development category, you might say, "To help other people realize their full potential as leaders."

After you have completed the list, rank-order your intrinsic motivations (1 being the most powerful).

MOTIVATIONS CAN TRAP YOU

Successive stages of leadership carry with them two contrasting challenges. On one hand, highly capable and experienced leaders are bombarded with increasingly attractive extrinsic motivators. On the other hand, to be an authentic leader, you must also be true to your intrinsic motivators.

Leaders are at risk of being trapped by their success. They may come to think that they are unable to live without a lavish salary, or fear that they face insignificance if they step off a public stage. They may fear that they have too much to risk if they pursue their dreams. These fears are traps because they obscure the fact that many leaders are not living fully despite their lavish salaries. Many who

Table 6.2: My Intrinsic Motivations

Category	My Intrinsic Motivations	Rank
1. Personal growth and development		
2. Doing a good job		
3. Helping others		
4. Leading and organizing others		
5. Being with people I care about		
6. Finding meaning from my efforts		
7. Being true to my beliefs		
8. Making a difference in the world		
9. Influencing others		
10. Other		

measure themselves by their public prominence are bedeviled by fears of insignificance, always measuring themselves against those they perceive as competitors. They may be afraid to follow their True North, failing to recognize the risks inherent in not pursuing it. The one-sided pursuit of extrinsic motivations is also a trap to the extent that leaders try to replace intrinsic motivators with extrinsic: trading wealth for satisfaction, recognition for excellence, status for meaning, and winning for making a difference in the world.

EXERCISE 6.4: AVOIDING MOTIVATION TRAPS

The purpose of this exercise is to identify potential traps—places where you might become trapped by an unbalanced pursuit of your motivations. To begin, consider each of the motivations you identified in Exercises 6.2 and 6.3. Examine the conditions in your life today under which the service of this motivation could become a trap. Start with your extrinsic motivations.

When in my life have I been driven primarily by my extrinsic motivations? What was the impact?

_____

_____

_____

_____

What traps related to focusing too much on my extrinsic motivations can I foresee myself falling into?

_____

_____

_____

_____

What are the things I could do to avoid these traps?
1. _____
2. _____
3. _____

When in my life have I been driven primarily by my intrinsic motivations? What was the impact?

_____

_____

_____

_____

What are the traps that come from focusing too much on my intrinsic motivations?

_____

_____

_____

What are the things I could do to avoid these traps?
1. _____
2. _____
3. _____

BALANCING MOTIVATIONS

Both extrinsic and intrinsic motivations are powerful resources for leaders. It is natural for human beings to seek recognition and reward, just as it is natural for human beings to search for meaning and connection with others. Both kinds of motivation are important to your authentic leadership when they are linked to your capabilities.

If, on one hand, you try to replace crucial intrinsic motivators with extrinsic ones, you can become unmotivated, dissatisfied, and even bitter. On the other hand, if you deny your need for certain extrinsic motivations, always serving the greater good rather than your own interests, you can become resentful of others' successes, vulnerable to being exploited, and anxious about your financial security.

Clearly you must find a healthy balance. The good news is that this healthy balance is also a necessary element of high-performance leadership.

EXERCISE 6.5: BALANCING MY MOTIVATIONS

What specific steps will I take to achieve a better balance between my extrinsic motivations and my intrinsic motivations?

1. _____
2. _____
3. _____
4. _____
5. _____

MY CAPABILITIES

Next you will consider your greatest capabilities—your strengths, if you will—and examine how you are putting them to work. The research done by the Gallup Leadership Institute, using its Strengths Finder, has demonstrated that individuals and leaders are most effective and most fulfilled when they are in roles at work that use their greatest strengths. These findings are reinforced by the positive psychology work of psychologists Martin Seligman and Mihaly Csikszentmihalyi. This work has launched an approach to leadership that places a much greater emphasis on putting leaders in positions where they can use their strengths. This is in sharp contrast to much of human resource development thinking in the 1970s and 1980s that focused on putting individuals in positions that would force them to overcome weaknesses.

EXERCISE 6.6: EXPLORING MY CAPABILITIES

In this exercise, you will explore your strongest capabilities and your developmental needs.

For this exercise, think of capabilities as complex tasks that you can perform with proficiency and ease. For example:

- Running complex processes with large groups
- Coaching several direct reports on multiple projects
- Gathering complex market information from qualitative data

Make a list of your capabilities. Then rank-order your five strongest capabilities *today* from 1 to 5, with 1 being your greatest capability.

My strongest capabilities are:

Capability	Rank

The leadership roles that maximized the use of my capabilities have been:

1. _____

2. _____

3. _____

From the roles you just listed, select the one that best reflects the use of your capabilities and answer the following questions:

Why was I effective in this role? How did I feel about my work at the time?

_____

_____

_____

_____

USING YOUR MOTIVATED CAPABILITIES

Effective leadership results from being in leadership roles that both motivate you and utilize your capabilities. One without the other is insufficient. Being motivated by something you are not very good at will not enable you to succeed as a leader, nor will pursuing a leadership role that utilizes your capabilities but does not motivate you. When you find a role that meshes your motivations with your capabilities, you have found the sweet spot that will likely maximize your effectiveness as a leader.

EXERCISE 6.7: USING MY MOTIVATED CAPABILITIES

In Table 6.3, list the significant leadership experiences you have had in your life, including those when you were young. Score each of them (on a scale from 1 to 5, with 1 being the highest) for the extent to which they utilized your strongest capabilities, and separately rate the extent to which you found these experiences motivating.

Finally, put a 1 next to the experience that was most satisfying in combining your capabilities and motivations, a 2 next to the one that was the next most satisfying, and so on for all the experiences.

Table 6.3: Using My Motivated Capabilities

Leadership Experience	How Much Did It Call On My Strongest Capabilities?	How Much Did It Draw Out My Most Powerful Motivations?	How Effectively Did It Use My Motivations and Capabilities?

After completing this table, write some notes about the experience that used your motivations and capabilities most effectively.

What stands out about this experience for me?

_____

_____

What did that experience lead to next in my leadership journey?

_____

_____

FINDING YOUR SWEET SPOT

Aligning your greatest capabilities with your most powerful motivations is like flying with a tailwind, paddling with a current, cycling downhill, or driving with high-octane fuel. It is the same state that others call being in the groove. We call the place where your capabilities and motivations come together the "sweet spot," after the place on a baseball bat, tennis racquet, or golf driver where the most power is transmitted from your swing to the ball. When you hit in the sweet spot you know it, even before you start to track the path of the ball.

Your experience is a powerful diagnostic tool for learning where you will excel in the future.

EXERCISE 6.8: EXAMINING MY CURRENT LEADERSHIP EXPERIENCES

This exercise turns to your present leadership environment. In Table 6.4, list the different situations in which you currently operate in a leadership capacity. Any aspect of your life can apply. As you did in Exercise 6.6, score each of the experiences (on a scale from 1 to 5, with 1 being the highest) for the extent to which they utilize your strongest capabilities, and separately rate the extent to which you find these experiences motivating. Finally, put a 1 next to the one that is most satisfying in combining your capabilities and motivations, a 2 next to the one that is next most satisfying, and so on for all the experiences.

Table 6.4: Finding My Sweet Spot

Current Leadership Situation	How Much Does It Call On My Strongest Capabilities?	How Much Does It Draw Out My Most Powerful Motivations?	How Effectively Does It Use My Motivations and Capabilities?

EXERCISE 6.9: FINDING MY SWEET SPOT

Make a list of future leadership situations that would enable you to utilize your motivated capabilities, then rank-order them from 1 to 5, with 1 being the best use of your motivated capabilities.

Future Situation Envisioned   *Rank*

_____

_____

_____

_____

_____

MOTIVATED CAPABILITIES HOLD THE KEY TO YOUR EFFECTIVENESS

In this chapter, you have explored your motivations for leadership. You have also examined the challenge of balancing your intrinsic and extrinsic motivations. As humbling as it may be to find your motivations out of balance, it is through erring on one side that you learn what you need to do to remain in balance.

Next you linked your motivations with your capabilities. In doing so, you identified your sweet spot for leadership. The likelihood of success and fulfillment is far greater when you are operating in your sweet spot.

Sustaining balance in your motivations and alignment between your motivations and your capabilities is not something you have to do alone. The support of those around you can help you sustain this balance and find situations where you can excel as an authentic leader. The next chapter, "Build Your Support Team," is devoted to this element of the True North compass.

KEY TAKE-AWAYS

- Each leader has a unique set of motivations to lead.

- It is crucial to differentiate between your extrinsic and intrinsic motivations and to understand how they sometimes work in harmony for you and sometimes do not.

- You are at your best—working in the sweet spot of your leadership—when you are highly motivated and using your strongest capabilities.

- By understanding past experiences that were highly motivating to you and that utilized your greatest capabilities, you can learn to identify situations that will enable you to be most effective.

SUGGESTED READING

Buckingham, M., and Clifton, D. *Now, Discover Your Strengths*. New York: Simon & Schuster, 2001.

Dotlich, D. L., and Cairo, P. C. *Unnatural Leadership*. San Francisco: Jossey-Bass, 2002.

Garten, J. *The Mind of the CEO*. New York: Basic Books, 2001.

7

Build Your Support Team

*Having a support team around you can be
invaluable as a foundation for your leadership.*

In this chapter, you will examine how you can build a support team to help you along your journey, especially when you are facing great difficulties and challenges.

Leadership can be very lonely, especially when things are not going well and you have no one with whom you can discuss the problems you are facing. Whom do you talk to when you're feeling vulnerable and insecure? Or when you feel that you are at risk of being exposed as an imposter? Or when your ethics and values are being challenged?

Perhaps you fear that others will not maintain confidentiality, or will get so personally involved that you are giving up some of your freedom. Or maybe you feel that they do not understand you or even support you.

Leadership can also distort reality for leaders. With leadership come rewards, recognition, feedback, and appraisals. What you may not recognize is that these things are often presented to leaders with a built-in bias. Subordinates wish to curry favor with their leaders. Yes-men and flatterers are constantly willing to distort or censor what they tell leaders because they want something for themselves.

Even more pervasive is the bias that persists when leaders are among honest and perceptive people. As human beings, leaders are biased toward action, toward existing theories, and toward situations and people that are familiar. However, the leader's bias for action and decisiveness can have the effect of shutting down or suppressing new ideas or alternative approaches, as people fear challenging powerful leaders.

Finally, leadership is hard. It requires vast stores of energy and commitment. It will use up all the energy you have and still ask for more. Without a support team, leaders are at risk of burning out. At the same time, they must give as much to their relationships as they get from them so that mutually beneficial relationships can develop.

In times like these, having a support team around you can be invaluable as a foundation for your leadership. When you are most in need of finding direction, your support team helps you get back on track. It sits at the base of your compass, because members of your support team help you stay focused on your True North. Your support team keeps you grounded in reality, and provides the support, counsel, and confidence you need as you venture forth to take on challenging tasks on your leadership journey.

In the exercises that follow, you will be identifying the members of your personal support group. Right now this group may be a virtual assembly of your intimate friends and family members. Or there may already be ties among the members of your support group.

EXERCISE 7.1: HOW DO I BUILD MY SUPPORT TEAM?

The purpose of this exercise is to learn about how you have drawn support from those around you.

Looking at your life story, think of a time when you most needed support from others.

Who were the key people that supported me the most?
1. _____
2. _____
3. _____
4. _____
5. _____

The five most important supportive relationships in my life, right now and in the past, are:

1. _____
2. _____
3. _____
4. _____
5. _____

Identify the impact that each of these people had on your life.

What was the impact this person had on my life? What might have happened if this person had not been there to support me?

1. _____
2. _____
3. _____
4. _____
5. _____

YOUR MOST IMPORTANT RELATIONSHIP

Your support team should be anchored by at least one person with whom you can be completely vulnerable and open, to whom you can expose all your flaws and still be accepted unconditionally. It could be your spouse, significant other, parent, coach, mentor, best friend, or therapist. Often this person is the only one who can tell you the honest truth when it really matters.

EXERCISE 7.2: MY MOST IMPORTANT SUPPORT PERSON

The person I look to most in supporting my leadership is:

_____

This person is important to me because:

_____

_____

_____

I look to this person for support in the following ways:

_____

_____

_____

_____

_____

BUILDING YOUR SUPPORT TEAM

You begin looking for the anchor of your support team in your family because most leaders have their closest relationships with their spouses and family members. These relationships are vitally important because they often provide the unconditional acceptance that leaders find missing in the workplace. Family members can also serve as mirrors that enable you to see yourself as others see you, even if it is fairly ugly. Beyond enabling you to show up ready to lead, your family can be a source of inspiration, a place to try out your leadership skills, and a source of straight-talking feedback.

EXERCISE 7.3: MY FAMILY AS A SUPPORT GROUP

In this exercise, examine the impact of your family of origin—your parents, grandparents, siblings, aunts, uncles, and cousins—as well as your family of choice. The latter includes your spouse or significant other; your children and, possibly, your grandchildren; and your in-laws.

What role has my family of origin played in my development as a leader? In what ways have they helped me grow and supported me through difficult challenges?

_____

_____

_____

_____

_____

What role does my family of choice play in my life, and specifically in my development as a leader? What have they done to support me in challenges and offer me feedback for becoming a better leader?

_____

_____

_____

_____

_____

DEVELOPING A MENTOR

Have you had a particular teacher, coach, supervisor, or adviser who has been influential in your interest in leadership and your development as a leader?

This is your leadership mentor.

Leadership mentors are the figures in your life who help you develop leadership skills and build your judgment and confidence as a leader. The best mentors do not have all the answers for you. Instead, they have the ability to ask probing questions that broaden your perspective on the issues you are facing and serve as a reality test for you, especially when you are in denial, distorting reality, or projecting your personal problems onto someone else. As leadership guru Warren Bennis says, "Denial and projection are the enemies of reality."

What many aspiring leaders fail to realize is that mentoring relationships need to go both ways to be lasting and mutually beneficial. In this way, they can provide both the mentor and the person being mentored with opportunities to learn and grow while working toward common goals.

Don't stop at one mentor, and don't think that your mentor or mentors must have the ultimate answers to important issues in your life. You are unique; your best learning will come from multiple sources. Maybe these sources would seem to others to be incompatible, but the more diverse your sources of learning, the better. In the end, you have to make the final decisions about your life—after all, you have to live with them.

EXERCISE 7.4: MY MENTORING RELATIONSHIPS

The purpose of this exercise is to learn about how you have benefited from mentors in your leadership development.

The following people have helped mentor me over the years:

1. _____
2. _____
3. _____
4. _____
5. _____

Which mentor has been most important to me in my development as a leader? In what ways has this person interacted with me and helped me develop?

_____

_____

_____

DEVELOPING GENUINE FRIENDSHIPS

One of the first areas of life to be cut back by busy leaders is their friendships. When things are going well and time is short, it is tempting to overlook the long-term friends who have been with you through good times and bad. Friendships, after all, require maintenance, time spent together, and the cultivation of mutual interests. When your work is demanding more and more of you and putting strain on your family, where can you find the time for friends? These are the times when you most need your friends, because they will be among the most useful reality checks and sources of support in your life.

When leaders are doing well, they are surrounded by people clamoring to be their friends. Everyone is calling to have lunch or dinner or to come to a party or a ball game with them. At those times, many leaders find it extremely difficult to determine whether a prospective friend is the real deal. But when leaders go through a down period, when they lose their jobs or their families or are accused unfairly of unethical actions, those fair-weather friends are likely to disappear, leaving only the tried and true as sources of support, reality testing, and contact with the world.

EXERCISE 7.5: USING MY FRIENDS TO SUPPORT ME

How important are your friends in helping you become a better leader? Do you have friends with whom you can share openly the challenges you face?

My three most trusted friends to whom I would turn if I really needed help are:
1. _____
2. _____
3. _____

A friendship relationship that has been mutually beneficial over an extended period of time is the following:

_____

I made this relationship meaningful and enduring in the following ways:

_____

_____

_____

_____

Describe a time of trial or crisis in your life when you turned to a friend or friends for help.

During this crisis, my friend was helpful to me in the following ways:

_____

_____

_____

_____

_____

Describe a time when you have been helpful to a friend who was in need of advice or help.

I was helpful to my friend in the following ways:

_____

_____

_____

_____

_____

Describe a relationship that did not work out for you, for which you feel some degree of responsibility.

The relationship that did not work out for me is:

_____

If I had the opportunity to do it over again, I would do things differently in the following ways:

_____

_____

_____

YOUR SUPPORT GROUP

A personal support group can be one of the most valuable and rewarding aspects of your life. Typically, such a group consists of six to eight people who meet on a regular basis to discuss important issues in their lives. The group works best when a regular schedule and meeting place are established and the group has a program or focus area for each meeting.

Ideally, the group will rotate leadership for each meeting so that each member has responsibility for developing the program in advance, even sharing readings or exercises with group members to prepare before they arrive for the meeting. Or your group may choose to hire a professional facilitator to develop the programs and lead the group. (For further information on how to form such a group, refer to Appendix A and reread the stories of the support groups of both Bill George and Tad Piper on pages 129–130 of *True North*.)

Your personal support group can help you identify your True North and help redirect you when you are getting off track. By asking for their insights about you, you can engage them in helping you stay on course to your True North. And you can do the same for them, as all relationships must be mutually beneficial to be sustainable.

EXERCISE 7.6: MY PERSONAL SUPPORT GROUP

Have you had a personal support group? If so, describe its value and meaning to you and your leadership. If you have never had such a group, would you like to form one? If so, what kind of people would you like to have in your group?

My personal support group is:

_____

_____

_____

Its value and meaning to me is:

_____

_____

_____

_____

_____

I would like to form a support group with the following kinds of people:

_____

_____

_____

_____

_____

CREATING A PROFESSIONAL SUPPORT NETWORK

A professional support network is a loosely defined group of individuals who can offer you professional advice and counsel, as well as assistance when you need it. The important thing here is to seek advice from a diverse group of people who can offer you insight and perspective.

These are people with whom you have worked or attended school. They know your work well enough to give you sound professional advice. Often they have the experience you lack in handling many of the problems you may face. These days, people in your professional network can be located anywhere, as long as you are linked to them by telephone or e-mail. Because you met these individuals in different environments, they may not even know each other.

Many leaders view a professional support network as the by-product of their success, or as the automatic result of the recognition that is their due. However, this approach to professional support networks leaves many leaders in the lurch. *You must take responsibility for building your own professional support network.* If you wait for others to find you, know that you will be operating first from the context of their agenda for you. Who is going to speak for your interests?

In thinking about how to build your professional network, you first have to define your profession and think through what kinds of expertise you need to help you along the way in your work. Leaders do not have the same well-defined professional associations and identities as do lawyers and doctors. What is the leadership equivalent of the community of cardiothoracic surgeons in a major metropolitan area? Identifying people in your network from different organizations, functions, and businesses and identifying acquaintances with similar or complementary experience are the means by which you can build a professional support network.

EXERCISE 7.7: BUILDING A PROFESSIONAL SUPPORT NETWORK

The purpose of this exercise is to craft a plan for building your professional support network.

What would a professional support network look like for me? Who are some of the people I would like to have in my network?

_____

_____

_____

_____

_____

_____

_____

Use the following diagram as an example to model your ideal network. Put yourself in the center circle, then place around you in circles the names of the people who would form your professional support network. Put the names of the most important people closest to center, and others farther away. Add circles as needed.

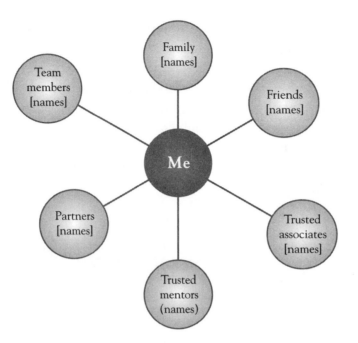

YOUR BOARD OF DIRECTORS

Businesses engage boards of directors to guide their leaders. Even privately held companies and family-owned businesses establish boards of advisers to counsel them. Would you like to have such a board to advise you about aspects of your life where you lack knowledge and expertise?

Your personal board of directors should be populated by professionals who can help you along the way. It might include your lawyer, financial planner, banker, accountant, tax expert, public relations specialist, and one or more mentors. It is critical that these advisers put *your* interests first—ahead of their own—and are not trying to sell you something. You should be fully prepared to compensate them for their efforts. If you solicit their input and take their advice on your own account, you will be well served.

However, you should be wary of professionals who are willing to advise you for free, or in exchange for your purchase of their services. In spite of their protestations, they often do not have your best interests at heart; examples of this latter group include stock brokers, plaintiff's attorneys, insurance salespeople masquerading as financial planners, and mortgage brokers. They plan to make money from commissions you pay, and are often inclined to sell you things you may not need.

You should consider forming such a board of directors now, not just when you are getting comfortable with executive leadership. A good group is an independent sounding board that will not only offer you professional advice and a check on reality but also hold you accountable for your goals and wider purpose. You can consult individually with board members or arrange to meet with them several times a year as a group to exchange ideas for you among themselves.

EXERCISE 7.8: MY PERSONAL BOARD OF DIRECTORS

The purpose of this exercise is to craft a plan for building your professional support network.

My ideal personal board of directors would include the following people (or types of people):

_____

_____

_____

_____

_____

How would I engage with my board of directors and keep them informed about my leadership?

_____

_____

_____

THE BENEFITS OF YOUR SUPPORT TEAM

In this chapter, you have had a chance to redefine your support team. Our advice is to think through the kinds of people you need on your support team and then build it gradually. With each individual, it is important to build trust and confidentiality into your relationship. Doing so takes time, but it will pay off when you need it most.

Remember, there will be many times when your support team will be the only ones who will tell you when you have lost sight of your True North.

In the next chapter, "Integrate Your Life," you will address the fifth developmental area of authentic leadership, that of being the same person in all areas of your life.

KEY TAKE-AWAYS

- Your support team is a necessary element for sustaining you on your journey as an authentic leader.
- Build your support team early. As you become a more powerful leader, many people will have biases that make them inappropriate for your support team.
- You have people in your life today who have been and should remain core members of your support team.
- Each phase of your leadership development should have a new leadership mentor.
- Assembling a personal board of directors can be a significant step on your journey.
- Having a support group that knows you and sticks together through time will help you keep sight of your True North.

SUGGESTED READING

Baker, W. E. *Achieving Success Through Social Capital: Tapping Hidden Resources in Your Personal and Business Networks*. San Francisco: Jossey-Bass, 2000.

Cross, R. L., Parker, A., and Cross, R. *The Hidden Power of Social Networks: Understanding How Work Really Gets Done in Organizations*. Boston: Harvard Business School Press, 2004.

Gladwell, M. *The Tipping Point: How Little Things Can Make a Big Difference*. New York: Little, Brown, 2000.

Krzyzewski, M. *Leading with the Heart*. New York: Warner Books, 2000.

Peck, M. S. *The Road Less Traveled*. New York: Simon & Schuster, 1978.

8

Integrate Your Life

The struggle is constant, as the trade-offs and choices
don't get any easier as you get older.
—*John Donahoe, CEO, eBay*

Living an integrated life enables leaders to be more effective in leading. It also helps them lead healthy lives and develop healthy organizations. Integrated leaders are able to make more thoughtful decisions and lead more effectively. Their employees are more committed to the organization, and therefore achieve better results.

Yet integrating your life is one of the greatest challenges you will face as a leader. To lead an integrated life is to bring together the major elements of your personal life and your professional life so that you can be the same person in all aspects of your life.

The grounding that comes with an integrated life helps you avoid being too cocky during high points or too stressed and agitated during low points. The vision and perspective that come from an integrated life are essential to sustaining high performance and to turning setbacks into opportunities.

Integrating your life is about making hard choices.

Take a moment and let that settle in. It is a message that may be difficult to hear, particularly for leaders who enjoy an endless array of opportunities and easy choices. You have been successful and you want to have it all—right now! If you do not feel some discomfort when you think about this, you may not be getting the point.

The kinds of choices we're talking about are not the endless decisions that appear to be the rewards as well as the burden of leadership. Integration involves saying yes and saying no to *yourself* on the basis of your True North. This is harder than you might think. When a plum opportunity comes your way with increases in income, power, status, and recognition, will you be prepared to say no? Put differently, will you be prepared to say yes to something important in your life and speak up for it? That's what leading an integrated life is about.

Well-grounded leaders have a steady and confident presence. Yet with leadership also comes the stress of responsibility for people, organizations, and outcomes—amid constant uncertainties.

Staying grounded will help you manage your freedom and your responsibility. The question is not how to escape from stress, but how to be in equilibrium in the midst of it. As one leader reminded us, "The state of zero stress is death."

We want to draw an important distinction here. Integration is not a code word for work-life *balance*. Balance implies adjustment to keep everything in one's life in a perfect equilibrium: "Okay, a little bit on this side and a little bit on that side . . . whoops, a little less over there . . . okay, now switch this for that." We've watched countless leaders try this balancing act and wind up dissatisfied.

The drawbacks to the idea of balancing are subtle but pervasive. Your attention is constantly drawn to the balancing act rather than to your life as a whole. With half-measures and adjustments, none of the aspects of your life is truly served. Perhaps most important, you are constantly moving back and forth between separate domains, carrying all the baggage of the different personae, responsibilities, and effort that such separation entails.

Integration keeps your focus on yourself and your True North. It prompts you to make honest choices about what you can realistically do and enables you to accomplish your goals. Even more important, integration enables you to be the same person wherever you are.

THE BUCKETS OF YOUR LIFE

Now it is time to examine each of the major aspects of your life: work life, personal life, family life, and friendships and community.

We're going to use the metaphor of buckets of water to represent the important areas of your life. Assume you have a limited quantity of water—your time, your energy, your spirit. You have several buckets to fill, but you don't have enough water to fill all of them. Do you fill each of them partway and monitor them closely for leaks? Or do you put all your water in one or two buckets to the exclusion of the others?

EXERCISE 8.1: THE BUCKETS OF MY LIFE

Let's examine how you can bring together all aspects of your life into an integrated whole in order to live your life with integrity. The underlying belief here is that in doing so, you will be a more effective leader and lead a more satisfying and fulfilling life.

First, you will look at your most challenging leadership experiences and your life today to determine which areas, represented by the buckets, need attention. (Refer to the bucket diagram in *True North,* page 140.)

As a starting point, we recommend looking at four buckets in no set order of priority: your personal life, your community and friends, your professional life, and your family life. Although filling the buckets in your life to the desired levels may seem deceptively simple at first glance, it is a lot more difficult than it seems.

Let's look at the status of your buckets today. In Table 8.1, begin by describing the amount of attention you give to each area of your life.

Currently, I divide my attention between the buckets as shown in Table 8.1. My desire would be to divide my attention as shown in the right-hand column.

Table 8.1: The Buckets of My Life

Bucket	Attention Given (%)	Attention Desired (%)
Professional life		
Personal life		
Family life		
Community and friends		

Note: The percentages in each column should add up to 100.

Which buckets do I need to direct attention to now, to sustain my effectiveness as a leader?

_____

_____

_____

Which of these buckets am I prepared to cut back on in order to make room in my life for one of the buckets that is too empty?

_____

_____

_____

What is keeping me from doing just that?

_____

_____

_____

Your family grounds you, no matter who you are and no matter what your relationships are with them. Your family members have a secret back door into your authentic self. Although you may at times want to tear that door out—as when your child's time table for your attention does not fit your scheduled meeting—your family members may help you get back to your True North when you most need it.

When you are at the top of your game and feeling like master of the universe, your family knows that you put your pants on one leg at a time and can't find two socks that match. And when you are at the nadir of your journey, they know your whole story, seeing beyond the present moment, and are there to support you.

You are not the first person to grapple with questions of purpose and values, working to discern the best reasons for making choices, and struggling to be a whole person. Spiritual and religious practices of all kinds have these activities in common, and you are surrounded by others engaged with similar questions. There is a wide array of resources that leaders can take advantage of. No one but you can determine which resources or practices are right for you, but leaders of all kinds tell us that they can use all the help they can get.

Your friends and community are important sources of grounding. You are more likely to encounter the diversity of life's experiences among a wider circle than your intimate family. By getting to know fellow pilgrims on their journeys, regardless of their economic position in life, you will become a more compassionate person and a better leader.

Start with Exercise 8.2 to begin to understand how well you are leading an integrated life.

EXERCISE 8.2: ASPECTS OF MY INTEGRATED LIFE

The purpose of this exercise is to design an integrated approach to your life based on the actual state of your buckets and the ways in which they sustain you and your leadership.

The most important aspects of my personal life are:

_____

_____

_____

_____

_____

How do I set time aside for myself and for my personal development? In what ways do I nurture my inner life?

_____

_____

_____

Consider the place of religious and spiritual practices in your life.

Do I have regular religious or spiritual practices? In what ways do they contribute to leading an integrated life?

_____

_____

_____

_____

Next, turn to your family life.

What are the most important aspects of my family life?

_____

_____

_____

_____

_____

In what ways will my life and time commitments change as I take on additional family commitments?

1. _____

2. _____

3. _____

4. _____

5. _____

How do I manage my family's time requirements, and conflicts between my family's needs and the requirements of my work?

_____

_____

_____

_____

_____

Turn next to your friendships and your community.

What role do my friendships play in my life? Do I look to my friends for regular counsel and advice on challenging issues I am facing? How much time do I devote to developing and nurturing my friendships?

_____

_____

_____

_____

Is my community an integral part of my life? In what ways do I serve my community? How does community service help me become a better leader?

_____

_____

_____

_____

In what ways would I like to serve my community in the future?

1. _____
2. _____
3. _____
4. _____
5. _____

Now turn to your professional life.

What will I do to ensure that I stay grounded professionally?

1. _____
2. _____
3. _____
4. _____
5. _____

In what ways do my family life, personal life, friendships, and community life add to or detract from my professional life?

1. _____
2. _____
3. _____
4. _____
5. _____

How will I cope with the seductions and pressures of professional life and still focus on my True North?

1. _____
2. _____
3. _____
4. _____
5. _____

MEASURING SUCCESS IN YOUR LIFE

As you practice living a grounded life, you should ask yourself, "How do I define success in my life?" Often the measures of success leaders use pull their lives out of alignment and prevent them from leading an integrated life. What measures do you use?

EXERCISE 8.3: MEASURING SUCCESS IN MY LIFE

The purpose of this exercise is to examine how you measure success in your life.

How do I measure success in my life right now?

_____

_____

_____

At the end of my days, how will I measure success in my life?

_____

_____

_____

Think about your experiences of happiness. Happiness is feelings of pleasure or contentment about your life.

What would bring me the greatest amount of happiness in my life?

_____

_____

_____

Think about your desires for achievement. Achievement is the accomplishment of goals that you have striven for.

What are the long-term achievements I would like to realize in my life?

_____

_____

_____

Now consider your desire for significance in your life. Significance is the sense that you've made a positive impact on people you care about.

How would I define significance in my life? What is the positive impact on others that I would like to have?

_____

_____

INTEGRATING YOUR LIFE

Integrating your life entails choices and trade-offs. You should make those choices and trade-offs in a way that fits your life and your leadership.

EXERCISE 8.4: INTEGRATING MY LIFE

The purpose of this exercise is to assemble a vision of your integrated life that fits your life and your leadership. Start with your experience of making choices and trade-offs between various aspects of your life.

What is the most difficult choice or trade-off that I have had to make in the past? What would I do differently in the future?

_____

_____

_____

_____

_____

What is the most difficult choice or trade-off that I am facing right now?

_____

_____

_____

Living and leading with integrity result from integrating your life so that you can be one person and be true to that person no matter what setting you are in. Think of your life as a house, with a den for your personal life, a study for your professional life, a family room for your family, and a living room to share with your friends.

Can I knock down the walls between the rooms in my life and be the same person in all aspects?

_____

_____

_____

Am I able to be the same authentic person in each environment, or do I behave differently at work compared to the way I act at home, with my friends, or in my community?

_____

_____

_____

_____

_____

FINDING TIME FOR YOURSELF

Leaders need time for themselves. Time, however, is perhaps the hardest resource to allocate to yourself. Nevertheless, it is important to develop introspective practices that enable you to relax and reflect on your life. These practices vary with each person. Some use prayer, others meditate or just sit quietly, and still others enjoy exercise, jogging, or walking alone. Because each of these practices takes time, you will need to be disciplined if you are to turn them into habits.

For many people, this chapter is the hardest of the book, but it may have the most important message of all in enabling them to sustain their authentic leadership. Remember, you are not going to find a perfect and steady balance. Instead, you should consciously choose the amount of time and energy you devote to each part of your life. Each of us will have a different mix that fits our values, motivations, capabilities, and current situation.

In this chapter, you also explored your own criteria for success, happiness, achievement, and significance. Applying these criteria to your life enables you to choose the appropriate amount of time and energy to give to each aspect of life.

In Part Two of this guide, you have worked through the five developmental areas of the True North compass. Now you are ready to move on to Part Three, which will enable you to put your authentic leadership into action.

KEY TAKE-AWAYS

- An integrated life evens out the highs and lows of leadership and therefore supports your authenticity as a leader in all circumstances.
- The buckets of your life are unique to your life.
- To follow your True North you will need to make choices and trade-offs between elements from all the buckets of your life.
- Each bucket of your life helps ground you in different ways. Each therefore helps you be more effective as a leader.
- If your criteria for measuring success in your life are going to fit your True North, they must also be unique to your life.
- Being the same person in all areas of your life is a necessary element for following your True North.

SUGGESTED READING

Albom, M. *Tuesdays with Morrie*. New York: Doubleday, 1997.

Gergen, C., and Vanourek, G. *Life Entrepreneurs*. San Francisco: Jossey-Bass, 2008.

Nash, L., and Stevenson, H. *Just Enough*. Hoboken, N.J.: Wiley, 2004.

Remen, R. *Kitchen Table Wisdom*. New York: Riverhead Books, 1996.

Part Three

Put Your Authentic Leadership into Action

In Part Two, you learned about the elements of your leadership compass. Now you will focus on using the elements of the compass on your leadership journey in order to lead with purpose, empower other authentic leaders, and optimize your leadership effectiveness.

9

Lead with Purpose

There is purpose in my work. . . .
At the end of the day, that trumps all things.
—Andrea Jung, chair and CEO, Avon Products

To become an authentic leader, it is essential that you understand the purpose of your leadership.

Many people want to become leaders but give little thought to their purpose. They are attracted to the power, prestige, and financial rewards of leading an organization. But without a real sense of purpose, leaders are at the mercy of their egos. They are ultimately vulnerable to disenchantment and even boredom. An even more fundamental problem for these leaders is that few people will want to work with them.

How do you discover your purpose? You cannot merely adopt someone else's purpose and still be an authentic leader. You can be inspired by others' sense of purpose, and work with others to pursue common goals, but, ultimately, your leadership purpose is unique to you.

After working through the previous chapters in this guide, you are now prepared to understand and lead from your purpose. Your purpose should be powerful, bigger than you, and evident to everyone around you. A true purpose drives you as a leader, gives you confidence during bad days, and keeps you from losing your perspective when things are going well. An overarching purpose will override short-term thinking and the decisions you might make out of fear of failure. Perhaps even more important, knowing your purpose will enable you to inspire and empower others around you.

There are individuals who, when they stand up to speak, cause others turn off their laptops, stop reading their PDAs, and listen with interest and even eagerness. These individuals lead with purpose and are able to communicate their passion. Having the title or position of leader is not enough to ensure that people will follow you or even attend to your words. There are too many distractions and too many inauthentic leaders for a mere title to suffice.

This chapter is about articulating your purpose—your True North—so that you are able to lead yourself as well as those around you. This chapter begins with identifying your passions through the lens of your life story—your crucible, the high points, and the low points of your life and your leadership. Next you will focus on defining your purpose and putting your purpose into action.

DEFINING YOUR PURPOSE

Many people struggle to find their purpose because they do not recognize their passions. For many leaders, knowing their passions and their purpose requires stepping away from prescribed roles and from the expectations that others have of them.

Yet in truth, your purpose as a leader has already been working through you for your whole life. If you claim your passions and lead with purpose, you can become more resilient and influential. You can become an authentic leader.

EXERCISE 9.1: DISCERNING MY PASSIONS

The goal of this exercise is to identify the essential elements of your purpose. This exercise will draw on your life story work in Part One of this personal guide.

First, review your life story, then answer the following questions:

When I was a child, what did I most love doing?

_____

_____

_____

When I was a teenager, what were my favorite things to do?

_____

_____

_____

_____

What did my mentors see in me that I didn't?

_____

_____

_____

_____

If I had no limitations on my life—no concerns about money, family obligations, or work requirements—how would I spend my time and my energy?

_____

_____

_____

_____

How does my crucible help me understand and define my passions?

_____

_____

_____

_____

How can I make a unique difference in the world?

_____

_____

_____

_____

EXERCISE 9.2: DEFINING MY PURPOSE

Using the previous exercise as inspiration, use the following space to write down elements of your purpose. Do not worry about the sequence of ideas or using complete sentences; just list your thoughts, impressions, and truths.

_____

_____

_____

_____

_____

Review your leadership values from Chapter Five, then answer the following question:

To align my purpose with my values, do I need to modify or add to the definition of my purpose?

_____

_____

_____

Now, collect those elements and write them in a complete statement.

The purpose of my leadership is to:

_____

_____

_____

_____

LEADING WITH PURPOSE

The more consistent your actions are with your purpose, the more authentic you are as a leader. In other words, once you embrace your purpose, you can bring that purpose to your leadership.

This is the true joy in life, the being used for a purpose recognized by yourself as a mighty one; the being thoroughly worn out before you are thrown on the trash heap; the being a force of Nature instead of a feverish, selfish little clod of ailments and grievances complaining that the world will not devote itself to making you happy.

–George Bernard Shaw, preface to *Man and Superman,* 1905

EXERCISE 9.3: LIVING MY PURPOSE

Using the definition of your purpose you created in the previous exercise, make a list of the situations or moments when you are living your purpose. Include everything you can think of, even if the event or situation lasts for only a short time.

Where in my life today am I already leading with a sense of purpose?

_____

_____

_____

_____

How did I feel in the most powerful situations I experienced when leading with purpose?

_____

_____

_____

_____

List some examples of situations in the future that would enable you to fulfill the purpose of your leadership.

1. _____
2. _____
3. _____

What am I going to change today so that tomorrow my leadership is better aligned with my purpose, and I am actually carrying it out?

_____

_____

_____

_____

_____

A LIFE OF PURPOSEFUL LEADERSHIP

In this chapter, you have looked through the lens of your life story to discover your passions and the purpose of your leadership.

Now that you have articulated your purpose, you will be a better leader because you know why you are leading. With this clarity about the purpose of your leadership, you can find others who share your purpose, thus building a community or team and multiplying the impact of your actions. In the next chapter, we turn to empowering other people to step up and lead by inspiring and aligning them with a common purpose.

KEY TAKE-AWAYS

- To become an authentic leader, it is essential that you understand the purpose of your leadership.
- By examining your life story and your crucible, you can understand your passions and discover the purpose of your leadership.
- Your unique purpose guides your leadership and enables you to empower others to step up and lead.

SUGGESTED READING

Autry, J. *Love and Profit*. New York: Avon, 1991.

Chappell, T. *The Soul of a Business*. New York: Bantam, 1993.

Coelho, P. *The Pilgrimage*. New York: HarperCollins, 2000.

Csikszentmihalyi, M. *Good Business*. New York: Penguin, 2003.

Greenleaf, R. *Servant Leadership*. St. Paul, Minn.: Paulist Press, 1991. (Originally published 1977.)

Renesch, J., and DeFoore, B. *The New Bottom Line*. San Francisco: New Leaders Press, 1996.

Warren, R. *The Purpose Driven Life*. Grand Rapids, Mich.: Zondervan, 2002.

10

Empower Others to Lead

*Empowerment means taking responsibility for getting
something done, and being willing to be held accountable.*

Authentic leaders expect outstanding performance from themselves, from others, and from their teams in order to achieve outstanding results. But high expectations and high standards are not enough to achieve these results. There must also be a climate in which others are empowered to lead and to assume responsibility for achieving the organization's goals and objectives. Authentic leaders empower others in their organization by aligning them around a common purpose and set of values and encouraging them to step up to lead. Thus they create organizations of empowered leaders at all levels.

EMPOWERMENT MEANS CHANGE

In empowering leaders throughout their organizations, authentic leaders can create high-performance organizations because all members are encouraged and inspired to reach their full potential. First, you must be an authentic leader yourself, and then foster a climate of mutual respect by treating people as equals, listening to them, and learning from them. To do so, you must be genuine in your interactions and encourage openness and authenticity in conversations. You must expect—not just endure—debate and constructive criticism as you empower your teammates.

Being an authentic leader requires you to have the hard conversations that give others the knowledge, courage, and confidence to step up and lead. Empowered leaders will continue to step up because they have the confidence that they will be supported, even if things do not work out well. As an empowering leader, you must help others recognize their unique gifts while also creating an environment that rewards those gifts in action.

Thus you create the climate in which others around you are comfortable engaging in authentic conversations and assuming responsibility to lead. When you give other leaders the respect and responsibility to lead, and create a climate of trust, they will be accountable for results and willing to align their actions around a shared sense of purpose.

These are the necessary steps you must take to change the culture of your organization. Only then can changes in the culture spread through your organization, as empowered leaders empower new leaders, and the organization earns wider recognition for its achievements.

Empowerment Comes *with* Responsibility

Early in my time at Medtronic, I made a point of talking a great deal about empowerment. Yet when I challenged people's plans and asked why they were not meeting their performance commitments, I received feedback that my questions and challenges were not empowering.

I thought hard about this, wondering what was required to get people to *take* responsibility for meeting their goals rather than *resisting* accountability. It turned out to be a matter of engaging them in authentic conversations. At a management meeting, I explained that an integral component of empowerment was taking accountability for achieving results. In the end, one of my critics said, "Now we understand you better. You're talking about empowerment *with* responsibility." The words were the same, but now there was a shared understanding of what those words meant and an acceptance of the importance of being held accountable for outcomes, not just effort.

–Bill George

EXERCISE 10.1: WHAT HAVE I LEARNED ABOUT EMPOWERMENT?

The purpose of this exercise is to learn from your experiences of being empowered as a leader and of empowering others. To answer the next questions, think about the best leaders you have worked for in your life.

What did these leaders communicate about my potential to lead?

_____
_____
_____

When I did not perform well, what did they say or do?

_____
_____
_____

What impact did they have on me?

_____
_____
_____

Now let's turn to situations where you have successfully empowered others.

When have I been successful in empowering others?

_____
_____
_____
_____
_____

What did I do that others found to be empowering? What were the outcomes?

_____

_____

_____

_____

Describe one or more situations in which you were *not* effective in empowering others.

I was less effective in empowering others in the following situation:

_____

_____

_____

What prevented me from empowering others was:

_____

_____

_____

Knowing what I know now, what would I do differently in a similar situation?

_____

_____

_____

SIX APPROACHES TO EMPOWERMENT

We learned through our research that authentic leaders use several approaches to empower people around them to perform at their highest level and help them discover their own True North. This chapter introduces you to six of these approaches:

1. Sharing stories about your leadership and your life
2. Helping others to live their purpose

3. Aligning everyone in your organization around a shared purpose

4. Challenging people to stretch

5. Sharing the credit with others

6. Meeting commitments by empowering others

In the following exercises you will put these approaches into practice.

Sharing Your Stories

One of the most effective ways to break down barriers and create a deeper level of trust and honesty is to talk about the challenging experiences you have faced, the times when you have made mistakes or failed, and how you learned from these times to succeed in the future. By admitting your mistakes and explaining what you learned from them, you give others permission to do the same.

EXERCISE 10.2: SHARING MY STORY

The goal of this exercise is to share all or part of your leadership story with someone else. Sharing your story builds meaningful connections and may encourage others to share their stories as well.

Select a colleague or close friend and share your leadership story with him. After you have finished, ask this person to share his leadership story with you.

What did I learn from this experience?

_____

_____

_____

What did I learn from hearing this person's story?

_____

_____

_____

Helping Others Live Their Purpose

If you are going to inspire others to take on difficult challenges, it is important to help them understand their purpose. In so doing, you can empower them to live it through their actions.

EXERCISE 10.3: EMPOWERING OTHERS TO FULFILL THEIR PURPOSE

The goal of this exercise is to discover ways you can help others understand their purpose and encourage them to realize it. Begin this exercise by talking with a subordinate or colleague about his passions and the purpose of his leadership.

How did I help him by having this conversation?

_____

_____

_____

_____

Aligning Others Around a Shared Purpose

One of the greatest challenges leaders have is to align the people on their team or in their organization around a common purpose that is consistent with the overall mission of the organization. One of the ways to improve alignment is through sharing your personal story of why the organization's purpose and values are meaningful to you, explaining how they fit with your purpose and values, and inviting others to do the same.

Engaging others around you in conversations about purpose and values can inspire your entire team to fulfill the organization's purpose. Your teammates will become more committed to living by those values. In the twenty-first century, the saying "People support what they help create" is truer than ever.

EXERCISE 10.4: ALIGNING OTHERS AROUND A SHARED PURPOSE

The purpose of this exercise is to explore how you can align people around a common purpose. Your challenge is to help those around you connect their purpose and values with the purpose and values of your team or organization.

What is the connection between my purpose and the purpose of my organization?

_____

_____

_____

How have I been able in the past to inspire others around a common purpose and set of values?

_____

_____

_____

_____

What specific steps will I take to create alignment in my organization around shared purpose and values?

_____

_____

_____

_____

_____

Challenging People to Stretch

In order to inspire others to stretch themselves, authentic leaders should match their high expectations with a commitment to reward success and protect others from disproportionate consequences of failure. We all know that some efforts fail despite the right purpose, the best resources, and good leadership. We have also seen the impact of leaders who reframe the story of a failure, recognize the achievements of other leaders who were a part of that story, and champion the lessons from failure in order to achieve success in the end.

At the same time, authentic leaders recognize that emerging leaders in their organizations need to learn about failure and find ways to thrive in spite of it. They expect their teammates to share information early, both the good news and the bad. They also expect them to stay engaged and be accountable for fixing problems. Authentic leaders can mentor their teammates by using failures and shortfalls as opportunities for learning and personal growth.

EXERCISE 10.5: CHALLENGING OTHERS TO STRETCH

Good leaders challenge and inspire others to take on greater challenges by holding team members to high expectations within a climate of trust. The purpose of this exercise is to explore how you can challenge people to stretch and take on more difficult goals.

What have I done to help people in my organization and on my team take on greater challenges?

_____

_____

_____

_____

Which people in my organization do I need to challenge to a higher level of performance? How will I go about this?

_____

_____

_____

What will I do when the team falls short of challenging goals?

_____

_____

_____

Sharing the Credit with Others

Authentic leaders share credit for success with all the players on their team. Conversely, when things do not go well, authentic leaders assume responsibility for their role in the problems rather than standing back and assigning blame. Nothing is less empowering to hard-working people than leaders who claim credit for excellent work and refuse to take responsibility for problems. Yet nothing inspires others to peak performance more than receiving their fair share of the credit for the team's success.

EXERCISE 10.6: SHARING CREDIT

The purpose of this exercise is to explore how you can share credit with those around you.

How do I feel when my leaders give me credit for a job well done?

_____

_____

_____

What specific steps will I take to share credit for success with my teammates?

_____

_____

_____

Have there been instances when I blamed my subordinates and teammates for the short-falls of our team instead of taking responsibility myself? What was the impact on my team?

_____

_____

_____

_____

Meeting Commitments by Empowering Others

It is not at all uncommon for leaders to feel squeezed between meeting performance goals and empowering others. When leaders feel that performance goals are slipping from their grasp, they are tempted to seize control from the very people they are working to empower. Yet often the problems in meeting performance goals result from too little empowering of others, not too much. It is therefore crucial that you use empowerment as a vehicle to meet your goals.

There will be times when it is both necessary and appropriate to step in, make tough choices, and direct the actions of others. When you intervene with honesty and out of necessity, you can maintain a culture of empowerment. Yet if you seize control from others reflexively and out of fear, then you may destroy trust and confidence in your leadership.

EXERCISE 10.7: HOW CAN I EMPOWER OTHERS AND STILL MEET PERFORMANCE GOALS?

This exercise explores strategies for managing yourself when you perceive a conflict between empowering others and achieving your performance goals.

Describe a situation in which you faced a conflict between empowering other people and reaching your performance goals.

_____

_____

_____

_____

How did I resolve the conflict?

_____

_____

_____

_____

_____

How can I empower others and still reach my goals in my present situation?

_____

_____

_____

What will I do in the next month to empower the important people in my professional life to be more effective as leaders?

My direct reports:

_____

_____

_____

My peers:

_____

_____

_____

My superiors:

_____

_____

_____

EMPOWERING OTHERS TO LEAD

Each of the approaches described in this chapter helps you empower others to step up and lead. Make a point of using the approaches that initially seem the most risky for you. By so doing, you will learn the best ways *you* can empower leaders around you.

Empowerment has many modes. Some authentic leaders are master orators, ready to come on stage and give a rousing speech to their troops. Others are adept listeners who provide support and a sounding board for their people. Still others develop every member of their team in ways that fit that individual. Regardless of the mode they use, effective leaders ensure that they empower others in authentic ways and foster genuine interactions among them.

In the next chapter, we look at how you can optimize your leadership style and use of power.

KEY TAKE-AWAYS

- Authentic leaders empower others to lead.
- To empower others, you must create a culture of authenticity, high standards, and shared responsibility through leading by example.
- To be an empowering leader, you must have honest conversations that build trust and engagement in your team or organization.
- Authentic leaders share their stories, help others live their purpose, align them around a shared purpose, challenge them to stretch, and help them get credit.
- Empowering other leaders helps you and your team achieve superior results.

SUGGESTED READING

Batstone, D. *Saving the Corporate Soul*. San Francisco: Jossey-Bass, 2003.

Charan, R., and Tichy, N. *Every Business Is a Growth Business*. New York: Random House, 1998.

Christensen, C. *The Innovator's Dilemma*. Boston: Harvard Business School Press, 1997.

Ferrazzi, K. *Never Eat Alone*. New York: Doubleday, 2005.

Gerstner, L. *Who Says Elephants Can't Dance?* New York: HarperCollins, 2002.

Kanter, R. M. *Confidence*. New York: Crown Business, 2004.

Kotter, J., and Cohen, D. *The Heart of Change*. Boston: Harvard Business School Press, 2002.

Lawrence, P., and Nohria, N. *Driven*. San Francisco: Jossey-Bass, 2002.

Lorsch, J., and Tierney, T. *Aligning the Stars*. Boston: Harvard Business School Press, 1989.

McGregor, D. *The Human Side of Enterprise*. New York: McGraw-Hill, 1960.

Rouse, W. *Enterprise Transformation*. Hoboken, N.J.: Wiley, 2006.

Sutton, R. *The No Asshole Rule*. New York: Business Plus, 2007.

11

Optimize Your Leadership Effectiveness

What distinguishes authentic leaders is the use of their power
to increase the net store of power in their organizations.

Leadership style and the effective use of power are two of the most important and widely written about areas in the field of leadership. Many leadership development programs begin with these topics, and some focus exclusively on them. Throughout this personal guide, you have been developing your leadership from the inside out, beginning with your story and continuing with the elements of your leadership compass. We have found that effective use of leadership styles and power must be built on this authentic base.

In this chapter, you will continue to build on this work. Self-awareness, leadership values, and motivated capabilities are essential building blocks for authentic leadership styles. We address leadership style and power together here because they are inextricably linked. Simply put, a leadership style is power in action, a dynamic relationship between the way you exercise power and the context in which you lead.

Authentic leaders can use different leadership styles while remaining aligned with their True North. The goal of this chapter is help you identify your preferred leadership style—the style that feels most natural and authentic to you—as well as other leadership styles that you already use or may want to develop for the future. When you understand your leadership styles, you can optimize your leadership effectiveness and more effectively use your power.

THE AUTHENTIC LEADER'S STYLE

Authentic leaders may use several different styles. In choosing a style to use, you should determine which style is authentic to you, suitable in the situation, and appropriate for your team. It is crucial to determine your teammates' readiness to respond to your style and the performance demands of the situation. The following list summarizes six core leadership styles. Review it and see if you can recognize your preferred style or the one with which you feel most comfortable.

Six Core Leadership Styles

- **Directive** leadership demands immediate compliance.
- **Engaged** leadership mobilizes people toward a vision.
- **Coaching** leadership develops people for the future.
- **Democratic** leadership builds consensus through participation.
- **Affiliative** leadership creates emotional bonds and harmony.
- **Expert** leadership expects excellence and self-direction.

In choosing a preferred leadership style, you should think carefully about the style that feels natural and authentic to you and about the way you feel most effective in interacting with others.

You may find that you tend to adopt another leadership style instead of your preferred style when you are pressured by time and performance imperatives, or when you find that your preferred style does not work. We call this a backup style. It's likely that you do not like using your backup style, but revert to using it because you feel that it is better at getting things done—in the short run, at least.

A superior approach is to master the use of several styles that are authentic for you, and to use them with consideration for the needs of the situation and of your teammates. For example, in a crisis you may have to use a directive style, but if you are clear about why you are doing so, your teammates will see the necessity of this temporary shift. Conversely, if you are managing highly skilled professionals whose knowledge in a particular area exceeds your own, a more democratic approach may be preferable.

Thinking about leadership styles has evolved in recent years. Earlier conceptions of fixed leadership styles have given way to an understanding of flexible styles. This shift in approach recognizes that authentic leaders adapt their style to the demands of the situation. Using flexible styles is likely to become even more important because of the increasing complexity of leaders' roles and the increasing variety of constituencies with whom they work.

EXERCISE 11.1: MY LEADERSHIP STYLES IN ACTION

In this exercise, examine ways to improve your effectiveness as a leader, including your use of flexible leadership styles.

Think back to situations in which you have been effective while under great pressure.

What leadership style did I use? How did I exert power and influence over others in these situations?

_____

_____

_____

_____

_____

How was my leadership style consistent with my leadership principles and values?

_____

_____

_____

How did I adapt my leadership style to fit those situations?

_____

_____

_____

How did I adapt my leadership style to accommodate my teammates?

_____

_____

_____

In the following situation, I reverted to my backup style under pressure:

_____

_____

_____

_____

How did results differ with this backup style than with my preferred approach?

_____

_____

_____

Did any negative consequences result from my change in style?

_____

_____

_____

LEADERSHIP STYLES CALL ON DIFFERENT SKILLS

To use different leadership styles most effectively, you must be aware of the skills each style requires. Table 11.1 lists core skills for each of the six styles. Examine the table carefully and see if you can identify skills that you might not be using in your preferred or backup leadership styles.

Table 11.1: Leadership Style and Core Skills

Leadership Style	Leadership Skill
Directive	*Driving:* marshalling resources and directing energy toward achieving a goal
Engaged	*Motivating:* identifying and addressing the desires of others
Coaching	*Teaching:* bringing others along a path of learning a new skill or domain
Democratic	*Collaborating:* responding to others and building on their contributions with your own
Affiliative	*Empathizing:* understanding the feelings and states of mind of others
Expert	*Mastering:* turning new knowledge into a domain of expertise

EXERCISE 11.2: MY LEADERSHIP STYLE INVENTORY

This exercise helps you identify the leadership styles that you presently use, examine where they are most effective, and identify steps you can take to improve their usefulness and effectiveness.

My *Preferred* Leadership Style

Leadership style name: _____

I prefer this style because . . .

_____

_____

In what situations do I use this style?
1. _____
2. _____
3. _____

Upon which leadership capabilities do I draw?
1. _____
2. _____
3. _____

When is this style consistent with my leadership principles and values?

1. _____

2. _____

3. _____

When is this style inconsistent with my leadership principles and values?

1. _____

2. _____

3. _____

What skills do I need to develop to use this style more effectively?

1. _____

2. _____

3. _____

My *Backup* Leadership Style

Leadership style name: _____

I revert to this style because . . .

_____

_____

In what situations do I use this style?

1. _____

2. _____

3. _____

Upon which leadership capabilities do I draw?

1. _____

2. _____

3. _____

When is this style consistent with my leadership principles and values?

1. _____

2. _____

3. _____

When is this style inconsistent with my leadership principles and values?

1. _____

2. _____

3. _____

What skills do I need to develop to use this style more effectively?

1. _____

2. _____

3. _____

Two Other Leadership Styles That Appeal to Me

1. Leadership style name: _____

I like this style because . . .

_____

_____

In what situations would I use this style?

1. _____

2. _____

3. _____

Upon which leadership capabilities would I draw?

1. _____

2. _____

3. _____

When would this style be consistent with my leadership principles and values?
1. _____
2. _____
3. _____

When would this style be inconsistent with my leadership principles and values?
1. _____
2. _____
3. _____

What skills do I need to develop to use this style more effectively?
1. _____
2. _____
3. _____

2. Leadership style name: _____

I like this style because . . .

_____

_____

In what situations would I use this style?
1. _____
2. _____
3. _____

Upon which leadership capabilities would I draw?
1. _____
2. _____
3. _____

When would this style be consistent with my leadership principles and values?

1. _____

2. _____

3. _____

When would this style be inconsistent with my leadership principles and values?

1. _____

2. _____

3. _____

What skills do I need to develop to use this style more effectively?

1. _____

2. _____

3. _____

HONING YOUR LEADERSHIP EFFECTIVENESS

As you weigh your teammates' needs and their readiness to respond to different leadership styles, you must choose the appropriate relationship you need to build. These relationships fall into one of three categories: dependent, independent, and interdependent.

Dependent relationship: teammates are dependent on the leader's direction.

Independent relationship: teammates act independently from the leader's direction.

Interdependent relationship: followers and their teammates establish a mutual dependency in which each is dependent on the other.

Dependent relationships are perhaps most clearly suited for inexperienced teammates, who may prefer a leader on whom they can depend and whose directive style communicates expectations with precision. Independent relationships, in contrast, are suitable for managing professionals, such as lawyers, doctors, and bond traders, who expect to operate independently and will only respect an expert whose opinion they value as much as their own. Interdependent relationships are becoming more common in complex organizations. In these relationships, team members take on their portion of a task while relying on their colleagues to do the same. They know that a leader works to bring the pieces together in an integrated whole.

USE OF POWER IN LEADERSHIP

All leaders use power, some more effectively than others. The more effectively leaders use power, the less often they need to use it and the more impact they have when they do. Yet power tends to be poorly understood, and leaders often do not realize the impact of their use of power on others. Table 11.2 lists the type of power used with each leadership style. Excessive use of power shuts down others' contributions, as when a leader's style intimidates teammates or raises the perceived stakes for failure. At the other extreme, when a leader does not exercise sufficient power or uses it ineffectively, teammates suffer in the resulting power vacuum.

Authentic leaders use power with attention to the likely results and possible costs. Table 11.3 list the likely results and possible trade-offs that come with

Table 11.2: Leader's Style and Use of Power

Leadership Style	Associated Use of Power
Directive	*Dominating:* to control the thoughts and actions of others
Engaged	*Influencing:* to affect the thoughts and actions of others through the distribution of information
Coaching	*Counseling:* to affect the thoughts and actions of others through the exchange of questions and information
Democratic	*Consensus building:* to bring together the thoughts and actions of others through building a shared point of view
Affiliative	*Supporting:* to affect the thoughts and actions of others through understanding and working together with their goals and beliefs
Expert	*Demanding:* to affect the thoughts and actions of others through setting clear expectations based on mastery of a task

Table 11.3: Follower Responses to Power

Leader's Power	Follower Response	Possible Trade-Off
Dominating	*Obedience* brings compliance	Acceptance
Influencing	*Empowerment* brings independent action	Control
Counseling	*Receptiveness* brings openness	Agreement
Consensus building	*Equality* brings agreement	Speed
Supporting	*Team orientation* brings teamwork	Clear vision
Demanding	*Autonomy* brings self-direction	Coordination

different uses of power. You can choose to practice consensus, for example. This approach may make your teammates feel more like equals, but you may experience difficulty in achieving agreement and meeting time commitments.

In another instance, you might choose to be tough and results-oriented. Such an approach can elicit obedience, but at the price of acceptance. Both approaches can elicit hard work and results from others in the organization.

When choosing among your authentic leadership styles, consider trade-offs like these in the context of the bigger picture. How can you use your power to increase the net store of power in the organization in order to obtain results?

Bill's Experience with Learning to Use Power Effectively

I learned about the use of power the hard way as head of Medtronic. In meetings with my team, I was often so driven to get results that I shut down the contrarian inputs from teammates who saw the pitfalls in my ideas. Thus I did not get the best out of them, and the group did not make the best decisions. Thanks to honest feedback from my subordinates about the problems I was creating, I attempted to restrain myself and to listen better so that others could be more vocal. This led to higher-quality decisions and better outcomes, as well as more fulfilled teammates.

In assessing my style, I realized that I underestimated my power and impact on others. Through introspection, I recognized that my drive came in part from feeling powerless on the junior high playgrounds when I was skinny and got picked on.

You must use your power effectively in leadership. If you don't do so, you risk underperforming, alienating teammates, and being dominated by other powerful people.

EXERCISE 11.3: HONING MY USE OF POWER

This exercise examines how you use your power and explores how you can become more effective.

How do I respond to powerful people who use their power over me? What is the most appropriate way for me to deal with very powerful people?

_____

_____

_____

_____

What role does power play in my leadership?

_____

_____

_____

In what ways do I gain power and influence within my organization?

1. _____

2. _____

3. _____

4. _____

5. _____

Describe a situation in which you exercised power over others when the stakes were high. What role did the exercise of power play in this situation?

_____

_____

_____

What steps can I take to learn to use my power more effectively?

1. _____

2. _____

3. _____

4. _____

OPTIMIZING YOUR LEADERSHIP EFFECTIVENESS

In this chapter you have explored your leadership style and your use of power. (Table 11.4 summarizes the discussion.) As you develop your authentic leadership further, you will find that your leadership style will evolve naturally. Teammates and other leaders will recognize that your style is authentic and will therefore trust your leadership.

As an effective leader who builds trust, you will find that your teams perform better. You will acquire greater influence in your larger organization and in the external world. (This virtuous cycle, as diagramed on page 152 of *True North*, leads to sustainable results and success.)

Organizations that follow this virtuous cycle produce leaders at all levels who are capable of achieving sustained results, even through the most challenging of times.

Table 11.4: Summary of Leadership Styles and Power

Leader's Style	Associated Use of Power	Leadership Skill Used	Follower's Response	Relationship Established
Directive	Dominating	Driving	Obedience	Dependent
Engaged	Influencing	Motivating	Empowerment	Interdependent
Coaching	Counseling	Teaching	Receptiveness	Interdependent
Democratic	Consensus building	Collaborating	Equality	Interdependent or Independent
Affiliative	Supporting	Empathizing	Team orientation	Interdependent
Expert	Demanding	Mastering	Autonomy	Independent

In the next chapter, you will create your Personal Leadership Development Plan, the final step in this personal guide. You will synthesize the work you have done and plan the next steps of your leadership journey.

KEY TAKE-AWAYS

- The effective use of style and power in leadership *must* be built from an authentic base.
- Leaders often underestimate their impact on others around them.
- Your leadership style can vary depending on the situation even as you remain consistent with your True North.
- Your preferred leadership style can be effective in many different situations.
- Your backup leadership style may not be effective and may engender distrust.
- Being able to use different styles flexibly will become more important with the increasing complexity of your job and the growing variety of constituents with whom you work.
- Authentic leaders are distinguished by their use of power to increase the net store of power in their organizations.

SUGGESTED READING

Bossidy, L., and Charan, R. *Execution*. New York: Crown Business, 2002.

Bower, J. *The CEO Within*. Boston: Harvard Business School Press, 2007.

Collins, J., and Porras, J. *Built to Last*. New York: HarperCollins, 1994.

De Pree, M. *Leadership Is an Art*. New York: Doubleday, 1990.

Heifetz, R., and Linsky, M. *Leadership on the Line*. Boston: Harvard Business School Press, 2002.

Lorsch, J. *Pawns or Potentates*. Boston: Harvard Business School Press, 1989.

Pfeffer, J. *Managing with Power*. Boston: Harvard Business School Press, 1992.

Useem, M. *Leading Up*. New York: Crown Business, 2001.

Whitehead, J. *A Life in Leadership*. New York: Basic, 2005.

12

Create Your Personal Leadership Development Plan

Only your vision of the future can direct you
on the rest of your journey.

There is a legacy that only you have the potential to fulfill.

Having completed the exercises in this journey to discover your authentic leadership, you are now ready to put them all together and create *your* Personal Leadership Development Plan (PLDP). Your PLDP is the culmination of this book. It captures your development plan with key actions that will guide your development as a leader.

Your PLDP should be a dynamic document that you revisit from time to time to assess the progress you are making in your leadership development. Just as you are constantly learning from your experiences and growing as a leader, so must your PLDP be updated to show your progress on your journey, to document what you have learned about your leadership, and to create the new paths you would like to follow.

In this sense, the PLDP is no different from a strategic plan for your organization. The vision and goals are clear, but the details of the strategy to achieve those goals must be updated based on experience and new information that becomes available.

Although the PLDP is the final step in this personal guide, for you it is just a milestone en route to becoming an authentic leader. You are like an explorer who knows where he wants to go but is constantly incorporating new aspects of the unknown terrain he is traversing. Your map for the journey needs updating to incorporate new discoveries, and your planned route needs adjusting to find ways around the obstacles you have encountered. You constantly refer to your True North and your compass to help you stay on track and to adapt when you find you are off course.

The essential thing here is that this is *your* PLDP, not one that has been handed to you by a consultant or a teacher. You own your plan, you know its truth for you, and only you can decide how and when to adapt your plan to stay aligned with your True North.

Although this is the concluding chapter of this personal guide, it is not the destination. Discovering your authentic leadership is not an achievement. There is no final state that allows you simply to close the book and move on to other

> When the jazz trumpet player Wynton Marsalis—recently named one of America's Best Leaders by *U.S. News and World Report* magazine—once asked his father what the key was to being a world-class musician, his father said, "You have to do the one thing that no one else does: practice every day."

projects. Authentic leadership is the path you are on. You will always face new tests of your values and motivations. You will face endless opportunities to be sidetracked from your purpose. The more you develop your authentic leadership, the greater the potential distractions, but the more opportunities you will find to deepen your commitment to your True North.

Your challenge now is to step up, articulate your vision of your True North, and design your development plan. Otherwise, this will be another of many books on your shelf reminding you of who you could have been.

EXERCISE 12.1: MY PERSONAL LEADERSHIP DEVELOPMENT PLAN

As you continue to build your self-awareness, you will find that continuing to develop a healthy mind and body will serve you well. Begin your plan with a foundation for yourself.

MY PERSONAL LEADERSHIP DEVELOPMENT PLAN

I. Intellectual Development

Where will I deepen my mind?

1. _____
2. _____
3. _____

Where will I broaden my mind?

1. _____
2. _____
3. _____

What areas will I discover through reading?

1. _____
2. _____
3. _____

What places would I like to live in or visit?

1. _____
2. _____
3. _____

II. Personal Discipline and Stress Management

What will I do to eat more healthfully?

1. _____
2. _____
3. _____

What will I do to get better exercise?

1. _____
2. _____
3. _____

What will I do to develop consistent sleep patterns?

1. _____
2. _____
3. _____

Which practices will I develop to better manage stress?

Practice	Notes
Meditating or sitting quietly	
Running, walking, or working out	
Yoga or similar practice	
Prayer or reflection	
Talking to spouse, friend, or mentor	
Listening to music	
Watching TV or going to movies	
Other:	

III. Values, Leadership Principles, and Ethical Boundaries

Review your core values, leadership principles, and ethical boundaries, which you worked on in Chapter Five, and update them here. Then rank them in order of importance. Mark those that are inviolate with an asterisk.

What values are most important to me?

Value Name	Value Definition	Rank

What are the principles on which I base my leadership?

Value Name	Leadership Principle

What are the ethical boundaries that will guide my professional life?

Ethical Boundaries

1. _____
2. _____
3. _____
4. _____
5. _____
6. _____
7. _____
8. _____
9. _____
10. _____

IV. My Motivations

Review your work in Chapter Six and update your lists of extrinsic and intrinsic motivations and potential traps.

Category	My Extrinsic Motivations	Rank
1. Monetary compensation		
2. Having power		
3. Having a title		
4. Public recognition		
5. Social status		
6. Winning over others		
7. Association with prestigious institutions		
8. Other		

Category	My Intrinsic Motivations	Rank
1. Personal growth and development		
2. Doing a good job		
3. Helping others		
4. Leading and organizing others		
5. Being with people I care about		
6. Finding meaning from my efforts		
7. Being true to my beliefs		
8. Making a difference in the world		
9. Influencing others		
10. Other		

My Overall Motivations	Rank
1.	
2.	
3.	
4.	
5.	

Foreseeable Motivational Trap	What I Can Do Tomorrow to Avoid This Trap?

V. My Motivated Capabilities

Continuing with your review of the work you did in Chapter Six, update your lists of capabilities, developmental needs, motivated capabilities, and future situations that might enable you to find your sweet spot.

My Greatest Capabilities

1. _____
2. _____
3. _____
4. _____

My Developmental Needs

1. _____
2. _____
3. _____
4. _____

My Motivated Capabilities

1. _____
2. _____
3. _____
4. _____

Future Situations to Find My Sweet Spot   *Rank*

_____

_____

_____

_____

VI. Personal Reflections

To be reflective or introspective, I will:

_____

_____

_____

(Optional) For my spiritual or religious practice, I will:

_____

_____

_____

To strengthen these practices, I plan to:

_____

_____

_____

If I do not believe in such practices, how do I confront the existential questions of life?

_____

_____

_____

VII. Building Relationships

The most important people in my life are:

1. _____

2. _____

3. _____

4. _____

5. _____

The people with whom I feel I can be completely open are:

1. _____

2. _____

3. _____

When distressed, I turn to:

_____

For personal friends to whom I can look for counsel and advice, I turn to:

1. _____

2. _____

3. _____

For professional advice and counsel, I turn to:

1. _____

2. _____

3. _____

My mentors are:

1. _____

2. _____

3. _____

My professional network includes:

1. _____

2. _____

3. _____

4. _____

5. _____

My personal board of directors includes:

1. _____

2. _____

3. _____

4. _____

5. _____

VIII. Integration

To integrate my personal life, family life, friendships, and community life with my professional life to become a better leader, I plan to do the following:

1. _____
2. _____
3. _____

To achieve my professional and personal goals, I am prepared to make the following sacrifices and trade-offs:

1. _____
2. _____
3. _____

IX. Leadership Style

My preferred leadership style is:

_____

Under pressure, I often revert to the following leadership style:

_____

My flexible leadership styles are:

_____

When dealing directly with very powerful or intimidating people, I:

_____

When exerting power over others, I:

_____

X. Leadership Development

The experiences I need in order to develop my leadership include:

1. _____
2. _____
3. _____
4. _____
5. _____

XI. Leadership Purpose and Legacy

The purpose of my leadership is:

_____
_____
_____
_____
_____

Being a leader relates to the whole of my life because:

_____
_____
_____
_____
_____

I would like to leave the following legacy for . . .

My family:

_____
_____
_____
_____

My career:

_____

_____

_____

_____

My friends:

_____

_____

_____

_____

My community:

_____

_____

_____

_____

At the end of my life, I would like to look back and be able to say:

_____

_____

_____

_____

YOUR TRUE NORTH IS ALIVE

Now that you have completed your development plan, it is time to refine your vision as an authentic leader.

If you want to continue to develop as an authentic leader, you need to balance your past life story with the story of the leader you are becoming. Many leaders stay the same year after year because they have only their past to guide them in the future. Your past, as you have seen, can help you find your True North. Only your vision of the future can direct you on the rest of your journey. There is a legacy that only you have the potential to fulfill.

EXERCISE 12.2: CREATING MY FUTURE

You are going to create a new path for your leadership journey. Take a piece of paper and draw a new path. This path starts at the present and continues into the future.

Looking forward five years into your future, call to mind your wildest dream of what you can become as a leader. On the path, make notes or pictures of elements of this dream or vision. Ask yourself, "What type of work am I doing? What role do I have? What unique gifts am I exhibiting? What type of impact am I having in my environment? What impact do I have on the people around me? What effect am I having on my organization or company?"

Add other major milestones, events, and changes in the path that need to be included to fill out your vision of the future. Now mark the path where years four, three, two, and one fall, and add any additional milestones or events.

EXERCISE 12.3: MY DEVELOPMENT PLAN

The goal of this exercise is to create the action plan to achieve your vision by establishing the next steps.

What is my five-year vision?

_____

_____

_____

_____

_____

Now examine these objectives and consider the next question.

What would I have to be doing one year from now in order to be on track toward these long-term objectives?

_____

_____

_____

_____

_____

What must be in place in three months from now to be on track for what I have defined for my one-year goals?

_____

_____

_____

_____

What action steps must I begin taking tomorrow to meet my three-month goals?

1. _____
2. _____
3. _____
4. _____
5. _____

Congratulations! You have completed your Personal Leadership Development Plan, your vision of your leadership five years from now, and the action steps you need to take to get you started.

SUGGESTED READING

Covey, S. *The 7 Habits of Highly Effective People*. New York: Simon & Schuster, 1989.

Grove, A. *Only the Paranoid Survive*. New York: Currency/Doubleday, 1996.

Kouzes, J., and Posner, B. *The Leadership Challenge*. San Francisco: Jossey-Bass, 2002.

McCauley, C., and Van Velsor, E. *Handbook of Leadership Development*. San Francisco: Jossey-Bass, 2004.

Afterword
by Bill George

Few will have the greatness to bend history itself. But each of us
can work to change a small portion of events, and in the total
of all these acts will be written the history of this generation.
—*Robert F. Kennedy*

Your True North is in sight. You have the ability, the tools, the motivation, and the passion to get you there. If you set your mind to it, you can change the world.

As the late Robert F. Kennedy said, you may not bend history by yourself, but by working with others and stepping up to lead, you can impact the world in such important ways that you cannot even envision them.

We face enormous problems in the world today. All human beings share a desire for global peace, the eradication of poverty, education, good health, and a sustainable environment. At first glance, the problems seem so large and intractable that we cannot imagine that our individual efforts could have an impact on them. But recall the words of anthropologist Margaret Mead, who said, "Never doubt the ability of a small group of people to change the world. Indeed, it is the only thing that ever has."

You can be the person to lead that "small group of people." These days the only thing missing is authentic leaders willing to take the risks to make the difference. As John Whitehead, who is featured in the final chapter of *True North*, says, "The world cries out for leadership." Will you be that leader?

Your leadership is needed now. Will you step up to the challenge? Will you empower other leaders to join you in your cause?

Ask yourself these two questions: "If not me, then who? If not now, when?"

When faced with such great challenges, our human tendency is to feel over-whelmed or inadequate. If you feel that way, consider the words of author Marianne Williamson:

Our deepest fear is not that we are inadequate.
Our deepest fear is that we are powerful beyond measure.
It is our light, not our darkness, that most frightens us.
We ask ourselves,
"Who am I to be brilliant, gorgeous, talented, fabulous?"
Actually, who are you not to be?
You are a child of God.
Your playing small does not serve the world.
There is nothing enlightened about shrinking
So that other people won't feel insecure around you.
We were born to make manifest the glory of God that is within us.
It's not just in some of us. It is in everyone.

Williamson, M. "Our Greatest Fear," from A *Return to Love*

We all have the gifts of leadership within us. Our calling is to use our gifts to make this world just a little bit better. Do not feel inadequate or modest. Claim your gifts and use them!

Leadership is your choice, not your title.

By pursuing your True North, your calling becomes clear. If you follow your compass, you can become an authentic leader who will change the world and leave behind a legacy to all those who follow in your footsteps.

SUGGESTED READING

Mandela, N. *Long Walk to Freedom*. New York: Little, Brown, 1994.
Palmer, P. *Let Your Life Speak*. San Francisco: Jossey-Bass, 2000.
Roosevelt, T. "Citizenship in a Republic." In *The Works of Theodore Roosevelt*. New York: Scribners, 1926.
Williamson, M. *A Return to Love*. New York: HarperCollins, 1992.

Appendix A

Ways to Use This Guide

Finding Your True North: A Personal Guide is designed to enable you to discover your True North. The sequence of chapters is based on *True North*, which should be read in parallel with this guide. Each chapter in the personal guide complements *True North* and builds on previous chapters in the guide.

The path to becoming an authentic leader is an individual journey. It must start with you. Yet you do not need to go on the journey alone. There are several additional ways you can get help in using this guide.

AS AN INDIVIDUAL

As an individual, you can do all the exercises on your own and prepare your Personal Leadership Development Plan. The more care you devote to the work, the more it will help you become an authentic and effective leader. Even if someone else had the answers for your journey to authentic leadership, the only journey that matters is the one you choose for yourself.

AS A MEMBER OF A GROUP OF PEERS

Many leaders find it is highly effective to work through this personal guide with a group of friends or new acquaintances. To increase the impact of your experience, we encourage you to meet on a regular basis with three to six other people to discuss what you are learning. Complete each exercise individually and then meet to discuss your work openly and solicit feedback from other members of your group. Members of the group can take turns leading and facilitating the discussions on a rotating basis. Please refer to Appendix B for more information about forming a Leadership Discussion Group.

If you are part of a larger group interested in working together, you may want to work with a designated instructor or professional facilitator, who shapes the content, guides discussions, and keeps the group on track. With larger groups it is still important to use three- to six-person peer-facilitated discussion groups. Many students in Bill's class at Harvard Business School have said that the Leadership Discussion Groups were among the most important experiences of their two years in the MBA program.

AS A MEMBER OF A TEAM OR AS A TEAM LEADER

If you are the leader of a team in your organization, you may wonder what would happen if all members of your team operated from their True North.

Being part of a team of people working to discover their authentic leadership and helping each other become better leaders through sharing their stories can be a very powerful experience.

You can use this personal guide with your team at work or in your organization, guiding the team through the process yourself or using a professional team-building consultant. (See Appendix B for ideas about building a structure for your team.)

AS A COACH OR MENTOR

As a coach or mentor, you may use this personal guide to guide emerging leaders through a process of discovering their True North. Each chapter is effective preparation for individual sessions. You can provide feedback and encouragement, and help emerging leaders explore themselves and their stories more deeply in order to access their authenticity.

As a mentor, you will find it essential to have completed each assignment yourself in order to be able to share your insights from your own journey. As a coach, it is unlikely that you will be sharing your own journey. Yet we recommend that you complete the exercises yourself first. For training for coaches, go to www.authleadership.com.

AS A FACILITATOR

The most effective way to create an organizational culture that supports authentic leadership is for a top management team to take the lead. As a facilitator, you are unlikely to participate in the journey on an equal footing with a management team. Yet we recommend that you complete the exercises in this guide yourself in order to fully understand the material and be prepared to work with your client's experiences. For training on this approach and information about how to help leaders become interested in authentic leadership, go to www.authleadership.com.

AS AN EDUCATOR

If you are an educator or a corporate learning officer, you may be asking, "How can I create a course in leadership development for my MBA, executive education, in-house training, or even undergraduate students?" You can use this personal guide and *True North* as the basis for a course on leadership development in either corporate or academic settings. The guide can also complement a course in organizational behavior, managing and leading change, or managing groups and teams.

The personal guide may be used with leaders at all stages in their careers, whether they are young leaders—including college and graduate students—midcareer leaders and leaders at the top of their organizations, or leaders embarking on the third phase of their leadership journey. The exercises and advice in this personal guide originated in our experiences teaching groups of executives and MBA students alike to follow their True North and develop as authentic leaders.

We recommend a twelve-week course format with three elements each week: (1) an individual assignment from this personal guide, (2) a six-person Leadership Discussion Group (LDG) session on each assignment, and (3) a plenary class that includes questions and insights reported out from the discussion groups and a case discussion of a leader facing similar issues. We recommend that

LDGs be allocated one class period each week. (See Appendix B, "Form a Leadership Discussion Group," for suggestions on forming these groups.) If there is time permitting for three classes per week, the last session could be split into two classes, one to generalize on the LDG discussions, discuss unresolved questions with the entire group, and lecture on the week's concepts, and another to discuss a case.

For in-house training or executive education, this material may be condensed into a one-week session, or may be truncated into a three-day seminar by eliminating most of the case discussions.

Appendix B

Form a Leadership Discussion Group

One of the most valuable steps you can take in becoming an authentic leader is to form a Leadership Discussion Group (LDG) that meets on a regular basis to discuss your experiences on the journey to authentic leadership. This personal guide is set up to be used for LDGs, wherein each group member completes individual assignments prior to group meetings and comes prepared to discuss openly his or her responses with other group members. The LDGs may take one or two weeks per chapter of this guide.

The typical LDG consists of four to eight people who consider themselves to be peers, but not necessarily friends, when they form the group. The key to success lies in all members of the group being open, willing to be vulnerable, and prepared to engage in honest conversations.

To make your group work effectively, it is crucial to establish trust and confidentiality at the outset. All group members must be sincerely interested in growing as leaders themselves and in helping fellow group members grow as well. To preserve the intimacy of the group and ensure that everyone gets adequate airtime, the group should not have more than eight members. It is also important for the group to agree on a meeting place and on the frequency of meetings—preferably a regular schedule of meetings in the same quiet, confidential place to help ensure full attendance. Both weekly and monthly meetings can work well, but in either case it is essential that all group members commit to being present at every meeting.

At each meeting, one of the group's members should serve as a leader and guide the discussion. The facilitator's role can be rotated to all group members, with each taking one or two meetings in a row. Alternatively, the group may wish to engage a professional facilitator to guide the group's discussions. In either case, one group member should check in with each group member every several months to determine whether group members are satisfied with the quality and content of the discussions.

The following is a model for a contract that LDG members should discuss and agree on at their first meeting. Modify this contract as necessary so that each group member is happy to sign the contract as an indication of his or her commitment to it.

Leadership Discussion Group Contract

A. Logistics

The LDG will meet each week [month] on [day of week] from ____ to ____. Meetings of the group will be held at _____.

B. Group Leaders

On a rotating basis, one member will be responsible for leading the group each session. The leader is responsible for both planning the program for the meeting and guiding the discussion.

C. Programs

The group should discuss and agree on a way to schedule assignment materials. The material from each session's individual assignments will form the basis for the LDG discussion. The exercises must be completed by each individual in advance, and then shared with the group by each group member. When the exercises in *Finding Your True North: A Personal Guide* are complete, the group should determine additional topics it wants to discuss in greater depth, or leave the choice of topic to the facilitator each session.

D. Norms and Expectations

The group should agree in writing on norms relative to (1) open participation, (2) trust in interaction, (3) confidentiality, and (4) group norms to support learning and each other, pertaining to respect for differences, expectations of tolerance, and ground rules for sharing feedback and constructive conflict.

[The following is a set of possible norms that might be discussed by your group and incorporated in whole or in part into your contract.]

1. Openness

To be effective, open sharing with group members is essential to learning. If individuals are not sharing openly with the group, it is the responsibility of group members to raise this with them for discussion within the group. However, it is important that group members not push individuals beyond their comfort zone on personally sensitive matters.

2. Trust

For the LDG to be effective, it is essential that group members trust each other member of the group and the group as a whole. Trust is built through honest, open communication and the sense that individuals care about the other members of their group and sincerely would like to help them in growing into effective leaders.

3. Confidentiality

A firm agreement should be reached that nothing said within the group is discussed with others outside the group, even with spouses or partners.

4. Differences

The group should allow for individual differences and make accommodations for what each member would like to get out of the group experience.

5. Tolerance

There are no "right" answers when life priorities or values are discussed, nor should group members make judgments about others in the group.

6. Feedback

Group members offer and receive constructive feedback from each other on their ideas, leadership traits, and communication styles.

7. Challenges

Challenges by other group members are considered to be healthy, if expressed in a respectful manner in which individuals do not engage in personal attacks. If managed well, respectful challenges contribute to meaningful learning for all.

Appendix C

Course Syllabus for Authentic Leadership Development

COURSE PURPOSE

The purpose of Authentic Leadership Development is to enable students to develop as leaders of organizations and to embark on paths of personal leadership development. ALD requires personal curiosity and reflection from students, and personal openness and sharing in the class discussions, leadership discussion groups, and one-on-one sessions with the professor. Leadership development concepts used in this course will be immediately useful for students and applicable for the rest of their lives.

INTELLECTUAL PREMISE AND COURSE CONCEPTS

The premise of ALD is that leaders who know themselves well and consciously develop their leadership abilities throughout their lifetimes will be more effective and more successful leaders and lead more satisfying and fulfilling lives.

ALD will provide students with many ideas, techniques, and tools to assist in their leadership development journeys, exploring concepts such as lifelong leadership development, leadership crucibles, discovering your authentic self, knowing your principles, values, and ethical boundaries, building support teams, leadership style and power, integrated leadership, and purpose-driven leadership.

BOOK READING

George, B. *True North: Discover Your Authentic Leadership*. Read this book in its entirety, preferably before the course begins, as we refer to its concepts and its stories throughout the course. (Optional: Read *Authentic Leadership*, by Bill George.)

LEADERSHIP DISCUSSION GROUPS (LDGs)

Each class participant will be assigned to a leadership discussion group with five other people. The discussion groups will meet for 90–120 minutes to complete the assignment for the week. These groups enable students to discuss personal materials in a more intimate group setting and to encourage a higher level of openness and reflection than may be possible in the class setting. LDGs will be facilitated by a member of the group, who will be assigned in advance. Each student will have the opportunity to facilitate for two weeks during the course. Facilitators will meet with the professor prior to the LDG, and will be asked to submit a summary of the group's discussion after the meeting, including open questions for the full class.

COURSE PLAN

Week I: Discover Your Authentic Leadership

Before the first class, write a one-page paper about why you want to take this course.

Personal assignment: *Finding Your True North*, Introduction
Readings:

True North, Introduction

Welch, J. "Get Real, Get Ahead," *Business Week*, May 4, 2007

Class I case: Wendy Kopp and Teach for America (HBS Case No. 406-125)

Week II: Your Journey to Authentic Leadership

Personal assignment: *Finding Your True North*, Chapter 1
> Reading: *True North*, Chapter 1
> LDG: discuss *Finding Your True North*, Chapter 1
> At the first LDG meeting, begin initially by reviewing Appendix B, "Form a Leadership Discussion Group," in *Finding Your True North* and establishing written guidelines for your group's contract.
> > Class II cases:
> > Howard Schultz: Building Starbucks Community (A) (HBS Case No. 406-127)
> > Howard Schultz: Building Starbucks Community (B) (HBS Case No. 407-127)

Week III: Why Leaders Lose Their Way

Personal assignment: *Finding Your True North*, Chapter 2
> Readings:
> *True North*, Chapter 2
> Peck, M. S. "Excerpts from *The Road Less Traveled*" (HBS Case No. 1-404-090)
> LDG: discuss *Finding Your True North*, Chapter 2
> Class III case: Richard Grasso & New York Stock Exchange (HBS Case No. 405-051)

Week IV: Crucibles of Leadership

Personal assignment: *Finding Your True North*, Chapter 3
> Readings:
> *True North*, Chapter 3
> Bennis, W., and Thomas, R. "Crucibles of Leadership," *Harvard Business Review*, September 2002

LDG: discuss *Finding Your True North*, Chapter 3

Class IV cases:

Oprah! (HBS Case No. 405-087)

Martin Luther King, Jr.: A Young Minister Confronts the Challenges of Montgomery (HBS Case No. 406-016)

Week V: Discovering Your Authentic Self

Personal assignment: *Finding Your True North*, Chapter 4

Readings:

True North, Chapter 4

Goleman, D. "What Makes a Leader?" *Harvard Business Review*, January 2004

Collins, J. "Level 5 Leadership," *Harvard Business Review*, January 2001

LDG: discuss *Finding Your True North*, Chapter 4

Class V case: GE's Jeff Immelt: Voyage from MBA to CEO (HBS Case No. 307-056)

Week VI: Values, Principles, and Ethical Boundaries

Personal assignment: *Finding Your True North*, Chapter 5

Reading: *True North*, Chapter 5

LDG: discuss *Finding Your True North*, Chapter 5

Class VI case: Narayana Murthy and Compassionate Capitalism (HBS Case No. 406-015)

Midterm paper: "My Journey to Authentic Leadership"

In your midterm paper, which should not exceed 1,500 words, describe the most important experiences in your life to date, including the greatest crucible of your life and how it has impacted your life and your leadership.

Week VII: Motivations and Motivated Capabilities

Personal assignment: *Finding Your True North*, Chapter 6

Reading: *True North*, Chapter 6

LDG: discuss *Finding Your True North*, Chapter 6

Class VII case: Kevin Sharer: Taking the Helm at Amgen (HBS Case No. 406-020)

Week VIII: Building Your Support Team

Personal assignment: *Finding Your True North*, Chapter 7

Reading: *True North*, Chapter 7

LDG: discuss *Finding Your True North*, Chapter 7

Class VIII case: Tad Piper: Crisis at Piper Capital Management (HBS Case No. 406-033)

Week IX: The Integrated Leader

Personal assignment: *Finding Your True North*, Chapter 8

Readings:

True North, Chapter 8

Nash, L., and Stevenson, H., "Success That Lasts," *Harvard Business Review*, February 2004

Hammonds, K. "Balance Is Bunk!" *Fast Company*, October 2004

LDG: discuss *Finding Your True North*, Chapter 8

Class IX cases:

Martha Goldberg Aronson: Leadership Challenges at Mid-Career (HBS Case No. 406-017)

Philip McCrea: Once an Entrepreneur (HBS Case No. 406-018)

Week X: Leadership Purpose

Personal assignment: *Finding Your True North*, Chapter 9

Reading: *True North*, Chapter 9

LDG: discuss *Finding Your True North*, Chapter 9

Class X case: Andrea Jung: Empowering Avon Women (HBS Case No. 406-095)

Week XI: Empowering Others to Lead

Personal assignment: *Finding Your True North*, Chapter 10
    Reading: *True North*, Chapter 10
    LDG: discuss *Finding Your True North*, Chapter 10
    The purpose of this week's LDG is to solicit feedback from other members of the group about your leadership and your effectiveness in empowering other leaders.
    Class XI case: Anne Mulcahy: Leading Xerox Through the Perfect Storm (A) (HBS Case No. 405-050)
    Alternate case: Marilyn Carlson Nelson and Carlson Companies' Renaissance (HBS Case No. 406-019)

Week XII: Optimizing Your Leadership Effectiveness

Personal assignment: *Finding Your True North*, Chapter 11
    Readings:

True North, Chapter 11 and Epilogue

Goleman, D. "Leadership That Gets Results," *Harvard Business Review*, March-April 2000

McClelland, D. C. "Power Is the Great Motivator," *Harvard Business Review*, January 2003

Gardner, J. "Leadership Development: Lifelong Growth," *On Leadership*

Whitehead, J. *A Life in Leadership*, pp. 107–111; pp. 275–281

LDG: discuss *Finding Your True North*, Chapter 11

Class XII case: John Whitehead: A Life in Leadership (HBS Case No. 406-024)

Week XIII: Your Personal Leadership Development Plan

Personal assignment: *Finding Your True North*, Chapter 12
    Readings:

True North, Epilogue

Finding Your True North, Afterword

As the culmination of the course, complete your Personal Leadership Development Plan (PLDP) and turn it in. In doing so, you should refer back to and integrate all the previous exercises you have completed in the course.

Final course paper: "The Purpose of My Leadership"

In your final course paper, describe the purpose of your leadership, and the principles and values that will guide your leadership. Discuss the areas of your authentic leadership development that you plan to focus on in the years ahead, and the steps you will take to become an authentic leader.

About the Authors

Bill George is a professor of management practice at Harvard Business School, where he is teaching leadership and leadership development, and is the Henry B. Arthur Fellow of Ethics. His new book, *True North: Discover Your Authentic Leadership*, immediately became a *Wall Street Journal* best-seller after its initial publication in March 2007. His earlier book, *Authentic Leadership*, was also a best-seller.

George is the former chairman and chief executive officer of Medtronic. He joined Medtronic in 1989 as president and chief operating officer, was elected chief executive officer in 1991, and served in that capacity through 2001. He was chairman of the board from 1996 to 2002. Under his leadership, Medtronic's market capitalization grew from $1.1 billion to $60 billion, averaging a 35 percent increase each year. George currently serves as a director of ExxonMobil, Goldman Sachs, and Novartis, as well as of the Carnegie Endowment for International Peace and the World Economic Forum USA.

Prior to joining Medtronic, George spent ten years each as a senior executive with Honeywell and Litton Industries. During 2002–2003, he was professor at IMD International and Ecole Polytechnique, both in Lausanne, Switzerland, and taught at the Yale School of Management.

George received his BSIE with high honors from Georgia Tech; his MBA with high distinction from Harvard University, where he was a Baker Scholar;

and an honorary doctorate of business administration from Bryant University. George was named Executive of the Year by the Academy of Management (2001) and Director of the Year by NACD (2001–2002). In 2004, George was selected as one of "the 25 Most Influential Business People of the Last 25 Years" by PBS Nightly News.

He and his wife, Penny, reside in Minnesota.

Andrew N. McLean is a researcher, consultant, and teacher in authentic leadership and authentic leadership development. His talents include assessing organizations and cultures for their authentic leadership potential. McLean was a doctoral research associate at Harvard Business School, where he coauthored more than twenty teaching cases and was also research director of the True North research project with Bill George. McLean earned a Ph.D. in sociology from the University of California at Los Angeles, and he teaches and lectures on the role of authentic leadership in managing change, leadership development, business ethics, and corporate social responsibility. His work has appeared in the *Harvard Business Review*.

Nick Craig is the President of the Authentic Leadership Institute (ALI), a training and consulting firm specializing in True North-based programs in leadership development, coaching, and executive team alignment. He has over twenty years of experience helping leaders create a strong culture of execution, balanced with high integrity, congruency, and authenticity. Craig is skilled at delivering programs and interventions for top teams and large groups, as well as at providing very focused individual coaching. His talent lies in his ability to integrate the work of Authentic Leadership with the achievement of sustainable business results.

Beyond his work with Bill George, Craig has been influenced by his work with Russell Eisenstat and Michael Beer, Director Emeritus of Harvard Business School's Organizational Change practice, helping top teams have honest dialogues that drive strategic implementation. He has also worked with MIT Sloan School to develop their Leadership Center and executive coaching program based on the Distributed Leadership Model.

Craig has designed and delivered leadership programs across the globe for many Fortune 500 companies, including BP, GE, and Siemens. Craig's work is documented in Ron Ashkenas's chapter "Beyond the Fads: How Leaders Drive Change with Results" in *Managing Strategic and Cultural Change in Organizations* (New York: Human Resource Planning Society, 1995) and in Ulrich, Kerr and Ashkenas's book *The GE Work-Out* (New York: McGraw-Hill, 2002). His client work with Russell Eisenstat and Michael Beer is documented in the article "How to Have an Honest Conversation About Your Business Strategy" in *Harvard Business Review* (February 2004).

How to Deepen Your Journey as an Authentic Leader

Our goal in writing this book is to support the larger movement focused on bringing Authentic Leadership to all types and sizes of organization. If you would like to deepen your understanding of this material and help bring it to others, we have a number of options available to you:

A. Contact Bill George through his True North website: www.truenorthleaders.com.

- Read Bill's latest articles and interviews on Authentic Leadership.

- Participate in Bill's Authentic Leadership blog.

- For requests to Bill to give speeches or conduct executive conferences, please contact Tom Neilssen at www.brightsightgroup.com.

B. Contact Andrew McLean at anmclean@comcast.net about research-related consulting or speaking opportunities and teaching True North–based programs in higher education.

C. Contact Nick Craig at the Authentic Leadership Institute website: www.AuthLeadership.com.

The Authentic Leadership Institute has been created to provide programs that help leaders deepen their experience of the True North concepts and materials.

- Speaking to executives on creating a culture of Authentic Leadership

- Public and Corporate 3-Day True North Authentic Leadership Workshops

- Customized Corporate True North Authentic Leadership Development Programs

- Top Team True North Alignment Process

- Future offerings:

    True North Train the Trainer Programs

    True North Coaching and Coach Training Programs